i ♥ cheesecake

MARY CROWNOVER

taylor trade publishing
Lanham ♥ New York ♥ Dallas ♥ Boulder ♥ Toronto ♥ Oxford

This Taylor Trade Publishing paperback edition of *I Love Cheesecake*
is an original publication. It is published by arrangement with the author.

Published by Taylor Trade Publishing
An imprint of The Rowman & Littlefield Publishing Group, Inc.
4501 Forbes Boulevard, Suite 200
Lanham, Maryland 20706

Interior Design by Piper Furbush

Distributed by National Book Network

Library of Congress Cataloging-in-Publication Data

Crownover, Mary.
    I love cheesecake / Mary H. Crownover.
      p. cm.
    Includes index.
    ISBN 1-58979-187-8 (pbk. : alk. paper)
    1. Cheesecake (Cookery)   I. Title.

TX773.C79 2005
641.8'653—dc22   2004030024

∞™ The paper used in this publication meets the minimum requirements of
American National Standard for Information Sciences—Permanence of
Paper for Printed Library Materials, ANSI/NISO Z39.48–1992.
Manufactured in the United States of America.

To my husband, Jack

I Love Cheesecake was only possible because of your loyalty, energy, hard work, and encouragement.

The above words spell **LOVE** for me.

contents

i ♥ cheesecake

I can vividly recall the day I met Mary on the way back to my office in the Nutrition Clinic. As we walked together, she talked excitedly about the cheesecake recipes she had been working so hard to perfect. She mentioned she had been bringing two cheesecakes a week over the last year for people to taste and critique. She invited me to participate in the tasting and evaluation—a task I was most easily convinced to do, as I love cheesecake! Still, I had to ask the question, since I had been teaching a great deal about weight control that day, how she remained so slender while making all those cheesecakes. She responded, as I hoped she would, that it was all in eating it in moderation and compensating for the extra calories by eating less in other places. It was so refreshing to hear this from someone besides myself for a change.

You see, I am a firm believer that there is "no such thing as a fattening food." You may want to read that over in case you did not catch it the first time. No food is solely responsible for anyone being overweight. Overweightedness is a complex issue involving total caloric intake as well as total caloric output through activities and exercise. You can maintain a desirable weight through the proper combination of both of these; this combination can include cheesecake.

Does this balance apply to those concerned about saturated fats and heart disease? I believe it most certainly does. A diet that has a variety of fibers, controlled calories, and choices high in unsaturated fats or oils will tolerate cheesecake occasionally.

With these things in mind, I hope you will enjoy the recipes that Mary has brought to us. As a cook, I appreciate and admire the work and dedication Mary has put into bringing you her cheesecake recipes. As someone with a modestly refined palate, I can guarantee you the recipes I tasted were delightful. As a dietitian/nutritionist, I hope you will enjoy these recipes as part of an overall healthy eating and exercise program. I think then we can finally put to rest the postulate that states "anything good is either illegal, immoral, or fattening!"

Rusty Foltz, R.D.
Cardiopulmonary Dietitian
Hammons Heart Institute
Springfield, Missouri
Formerly at University of Missouri–Columbia

a note from the author

Many of us share a lifetime enthusiasm for the great taste of cheesecake. We simply love this indulgence! Further, this dessert is the ultimate in glamour and sophistication, providing the "Grand Finale" to an elegant meal or social affair.

Where I grew up, most people bought cheesecakes at elegant bakeries, thinking them much too difficult for the ordinary kitchen. In this book, I will show you how easy making cheesecakes really is.

My mother is an excellent cook, as were both of my grandmothers. The skills they taught me formed the core for my desire to master one of my food passions: cheesecake. I began by first modifying a lemon-ice box pie. Later, I found recipes for "real" cheesecakes, which started me on the road to writing this book. Along the way, I began questioning cheesecake formulas. I challenged the concept of why one "cracks" and where the basic flavor ought to lie. Having experimented extensively with these recipes, in this book I am continuing to present new formulas for basic cheesecakes.

Cheesecake is the first dessert I worked on when I was creating the very first bread machine with a "Dessert Cycle." The bread machine has my name on the patent and was created for Toastmaster Inc. This wonderful machine is still available. I also created quite a few recipes for Toastmaster Inc. and their stand mixer.

Atlanta Georgia is my birth town, and I treasure every moment I spent there. I am the daughter of Burwell and Mary Frances Humphrey, and I have one sibling, a sister, Jeanne Reece.

My three children were raised in Columbia, Missouri, a nice small town in the Midwest. Columbia has a university and two large colleges. It is where I wrote *Cheesecake Extraordinaire*. I taught many adult education classes on cheesecake-making as well as other foods. For ten years I was a regular guest with a cooking segment on the NBC TV affiliate in Columbia. I have many fond memories of this.

Jack Gilbert is my (second) husband, and we have been married (almost) one year. We live in Punta Gorda, Florida, where the atmosphere is paradise-like. Jack was an analytical chemist for Merck Pharmaceutical Co., where he enforced quality control for process development of new drugs. With some fast-talking, I convinced Jack to help tabulate nutritional values of all the yogurt cheesecakes!

As you can imagine, I am thrilled with my latest venture, creating a new series of cheesecakes made from yogurt. These recipes, I am pleased to say, have a reduced cholesterol content compared to cream cheese cheesecakes, so they are healthier. In this book, you will also find some new ideas presented. But before passing judgment, try a few. I am convinced that you and your family will find many surprises. May you enjoy the experience as much as I have.

I sincerely hope you enjoy my cheesecakes.

Mary Crownover

acknowledgments

Special thanks are due to the many people who encouraged and supported me in the creation of these recipes. Their enthusiasm was overwhelming.

A special thanks goes to Rusty Foltz, R.D., for being a friend and for offering to write the foreword for this book.

I want to thank the staff of Charlotte Dental Associates for testing the recipes for this book. This group took their job seriously and was good about giving me feedback on my recipes. This project would have been very difficult without their help.

I especially want to thank my husband, Jack Gilbert, for being so supportive and helpful. Jack ran more errands than I could count. And Jack licked the bowl, beater, and spoons before the cakes were even baked!

Thank you Taylor Trade Publishing for offering me the great opportunity of updating my best-selling cookbook *Cheesecake Extraordinaire*. The Taylor staff is a joy to work with. Mandy Phillips, my editor, is a ray of sunshine; any author would be privileged to work with her. I must also include my production editor, Ginger Strader. She is fantastic and has pulled my book together for me. Because of her guidance, I have this lovely book.

success every time: history & hints

the history of cheesecake

Cheesecake history may extend almost as far into the past as that of cheese itself. Surely, not long after the happy discovery that milk souring could produce a tasty and high protein food, that product was utilized in the arts of cooking and baking.

The Greeks enjoyed a form of cheesecake nearly 3,000 years ago, recording that it was both a desired delicacy and a food fit for athletes competing in the Olympic Games. Thereafter, Roman menus included cheesecakes. The Orthodox Church utilized cheesecakes in its Easter tradition farther to the east. Record-keeping in the early Christian era, the Dark Ages, and the Middle Ages was sparse then rapidly expanded during the Renaissance and into modern times. That explosion of written communication allows us to trace cheesecake usage later in history. Samuel Pepys' diary in the seventeenth century and Hannah Glasse's cookbook in the eighteenth century referred to cheesecakes of various kinds and flavors, even as Europeans migrated to the New World, bringing those delicacies. Then, in the late nineteenth century, two New York dairy farmers developed fine cream cheese, perhaps inspired by neufchatel cheese from France, making it possible for cheesecake-making to reach its pinnacle of perfection. The new cheese was about one-third cream, rather than being a curd cheese. In South Edmonston, New York, the product was developed for the Empire Cheese Company and eventually became known as Philadelphia Brand Cream Cheese. In the last 100 years, cheesecake-making with cream cheese has advanced technically, but choices of flavoring ingredients have been limited by the compatibility of those

i ♥ cheesecake

ingredients with the structural integrity of the cakes themselves. Some recipes warn of the likelihood of cracking of the cake. However, in these pages I shall give several basic formulas that will allow you to make cheesecakes both with beautiful appearance and with a great variety of flavors and flavor combinations.

cheesecake pans

While it is more fashionable to use a spring form cake pan, I have found that a pan with a solid index and false bottom is much more useful. Regardless of the pan you choose, ensure that its construction is of heavy aluminum; the extra dollars will pay off in the long run. Also, be careful of tin-plate pans, as they have a tendency to rust.

appliances

MIXERS: A heavy duty mixer is the one luxury that every kitchen should have. It saves time in mixing a batter uniformly. Further, the beating produces a creamier texture in cheesecakes.

BLENDERS: Blenders are very useful for liquefying, pureeing, and chopping fruit.

FOOD PROCESSORS: A food processor comes in handy for making cookie crumbs (which is considerably cheaper than buying them packaged). It also is useful in chopping nuts.

MICROWAVE OVENS: A microwave oven saves a lot of time in melting butter or margarine, melting chocolate, toasting nuts, softening cream cheese, and making toppings.

GAS OR ELECTRIC OVENS: It makes no difference whether you have a gas or electric oven. However, accurate baking temperature is essential. You can easily check your cooking temperature with an oven thermometer, which can be obtained at most kitchenware stores.

ingredients

CHEESE: The cheese is the most prominent ingredient in all cheesecakes and so must be chosen with care. I prefer cream cheese, as it has a lower water content than Neufchatel (60%), cottage cheese (78%), or ricotta (72%). This, combined with its higher butter fat content, produces a creamier texture.

SUGAR: Use granulated sugar unless otherwise directed. When brown sugar is called for, pack it down when measuring.

CORNSTARCH AND FLOUR: In these recipes, I use cornstarch more often than flour, as it has a finer texture. Any all-purpose flour will work well, and sifting is not necessary.

WHIPPING CREAM: To whip cream properly, I recommend using a mixer rather than a blender or a food processor.

CHOCOLATE AND CHOCOLATE SUBSTITUTES: I recommend using real chocolate, as the taste and texture is less wax-like. It pays not to cheat on taste. For the same reasons, when using white chocolate, use a good brand. Real chocolate, or cocoa, are the purist's choice.

When melting chocolate, use only low heat, with plenty of stirring, as chocolate burns and scorches easily. One handy way to melt chocolate is by using your microwave oven. Place the chocolate in a microwave-safe bowl or container and micro-cook on 100% power (high) until chocolate almost melts. Remove from the microwave and stir until melted and smooth. Or you may follow the directions on the chocolate package.

When working with chocolate, start the process with dry equipment, as water will cause chocolate to stiffen.

Now for substitutes! When milk chocolate chips are called for, you may use milk chocolate bars of an equal weight. For semisweet chocolate chips, use semisweet chocolate ounce squares of the same weight.

NUTS (TOASTED): I frequently call for almonds or other nuts in my recipes. Toasting them brings out the flavor and crunch that people like and is surprisingly easy. Place the nuts evenly on a cookie sheet or baking pan and bake for 8–10 minutes at 350 degrees, stirring occasionally. For the microwave, place the nuts evenly on a glass pie plate and cook 5–7 minutes, stirring every minute until golden. The culinary taste rarely misses this treat.

EGGS: A hint well worth remembering is to never overbeat eggs, as this will cause the cake to crack. Indeed, a concentric crack is a sure sign of this common mistake. Large eggs have been used in all of these recipes.

GREASE: For greasing the cake pan, use butter or margarine.

helpful hints

- Make your cheesecake at least one day ahead to allow the flavors to ripen.
- Have all of the ingredients at room temperature before starting. By doing so, it is easier to achieve a creamy consistency. If you forget, or are in a hurry, warm the cream cheese for 10 minutes in the oven at 200 degrees. If you prefer to use the microwave, remove the foil and heat on medium (50% heat) for 2–3 minutes.
- Put the whole eggs in a bowl of warm water for 5–10 minutes before adding them to your cake.

MEASURING INGREDIENTS: When using a measuring cup, use eye level to read the amount. For a teaspoon or tablespoon, use the back of a knife to level the spoon. Accurate measurements are important.

TOPPINGS: All cooked toppings can be made in a microwave. However, be careful of overcooking them, as this will give them a rubbery texture.

UNCOOKED COOKIE CRUST: All uncooked crusts are crispier if they are refrigerated for a while.

OVEN DRIP PAN: Cheesecake pans have a tendency to leak. To save yourself from frequent "big oven clean ups," place a drip pan on the bottom rack of the oven. An old, dull or nonshiny cookie sheet works best.

HOW TO TELL WHEN CHEESECAKE IS DONE: Never overbake a cheesecake! It is better to underbake it. The center should look firm when done. If your cake has a "wet or shiny look" in the center, it needs to stay in the oven longer. Should you decide to do this, pull the cake out of the oven and run a knife around the inside edge of the pan to prevent the cake from cracking while it is firming up. Then turn the oven off and return the cake to it for an additional 2 hours. Cool the cake to room temperature and then refrigerate overnight. If time does not permit this, put it in the refrigerator uncovered. (Covering will cause condensation to collect on the top, which may produce discoloration in chocolate. If some moisture does collect, simply wipe it off with a paper towel.) Cheesecakes should be refrigerated for 8–12 hours before cutting.

SLICING THE CAKE: Slice with a thin, sharp knife.

CAKE CRACKING: There are several causes for a cheesecake to crack. Beating the eggs at too high a speed with a mixer will cause a concentric crack (one that goes around the cake). Always beat eggs only at a low or medium speed. Another cause is cooking the cake at too high a temperature. Cooking the cake too long will produce the "Grand Canyon crack," which can be avoided by meticulous attention to timing. Finally, cracking also can occur in the cooling process. As a cake cools, it begins to shrink. If it sticks to the side of the pan, it will crack in the center. Therefore, run a knife around the edge of the cake to separate it from the pan. If your cakes continue to crack after taking the above precautions, then buy an oven thermometer to check the real temperature at which you are cooking.

REPAIRING A CRACKED CHEESECAKE: Repairing a cracked cake is easy: just pretend that it is play dough or clay! After your cake has cooled, mold and shape it with a hot, wet, unserrated knife. You can smooth away any flaw with this method.

FREEZING CHEESECAKE: The rule of thumb for cheesecake freezing is "the richer they are, the better they freeze." All of the cakes in this book freeze beautifully and can be kept for several months. To freeze a cake, prepare it in the usual fashion, then freeze it on a tray for at least 6 hours. Next, remove the cake and wrap it in freezer-weight foil or place it in an airtight plastic bag. Then back to the freezer until needed. It is best to freeze the cake without the topping. Thaw the uncovered cake in the refrigerator overnight or at room temperature for 2–3 hours.

GIVING A CHEESECAKE AWAY: When giving a cake away, be careful not to include the bottom of the pan! Instead, cover the loose bottom tightly with heavy duty foil before pouring the batter into the pan. After cooking the cake and chilling it, loosen and remove the bottom of the pan. Transfer the cake to a cardboard disk, slipping the bottom of the pan out and attaching the foil to the bottom of the disk. These "cardboard disks" can be bought where professional cake supplies are sold, in the housewares departments of department stores, at hobby stores, or in pizza parlors. These disks come in several sizes. If necessary, cut them to the size of your cake pan.

garnishing techniques

CHOCOLATE CURLS: Use a bar of milk chocolate at room temperature. Carefully draw a vegetable peeler across the surface of the chocolate, making thin strips that curl. For smaller curls, use the narrow side of the chocolate. For larger curls, use the wide surface.

GRATED CHOCOLATE: Rub a cool, firm piece of chocolate across the grates of a hand grater. Clean the surface of the grater occasionally to prevent clogging.

SHAVED CHOCOLATE: Using short, quick strokes, scrape a vegetable peeler across the surface of a cool, firm piece of chocolate.

CITRUS TWISTS: Thinly slice lemons, limes, or oranges. Using a sharp knife, cut into the center of each slice. Twist the ends in opposite directions.

PIPING WHIPPED CREAM: Fold back the top of a pastry bag and spoon whipped cream into it. Unfold the top of the bag and twist closed. Gently squeeze the bag to release the whipped cream. The design is determined by the size of the tip you use.

modifying your recipe

This book is written for 9-inch cheesecake pans. With the help of a calculator, you can change any recipe in this book to your pan size.

Pan size	Multiply by
12 inch	1.8
10 inch	1.2
9½ inch	1.1

i ♥ cheesecake

Pan size	Multiply by
9 inch	1.0
8½ inch	0.9
8 inch	0.8
7 inch	0.6
6 inch	0.4
4 inch	0.2

inventing your own cheesecake

Inventing your own cheesecake is fun and rewarding. It gives you the opportunity to enjoy and show off your own creativity. In this section, I will give you the formula for altering my cheesecakes into ones with your own special touch.

The formula is simple:

Substitute a liquid for an equal amount of liquid, or a dry ingredient for an equal amount of a dry ingredient.

This applies to fruit juices, liqueur, and extracts. Of course you may substitute heavy cream for sour cream.

Interchanging fruits can be a little tricky; some have a higher water content than others. Try to match them as closely as possible for an even exchange. For example, blackberries, blueberries, and raspberries are interchangeable, as are strawberries and cherries, chopped apples and chopped pears, pureed bananas and pureed pears. Oranges, tangerines, peaches, and pineapple are also interchangeable.

Chocolate exchanging is a little more difficult. First, measure an equal amount or weight of the chocolate of your choice. Next, when replacing milk or semisweet chocolate with German chocolate, use slightly *less* sugar; when replacing German chocolate with milk or semisweet chocolate, add slightly *more* sugar to the recipe.

I do not recommend exchanging peanut butter or pumpkin for a different ingredient. Both are tricky to work with.

Dark brown, light brown, or granulated sugar in equal amounts can be exchanged.

As an example of substitutions, examine these recipes: Creamy Lemon, Lemon Drop, Key Lime, and Limon. Note how similar these are. It was easy to create all of these recipes by changing a few key flavors.

Feel free to also mix and match any of the crusts, cakes, or toppings. Let your imagination run wild!

beverage based

AMARETTO CHEESECAKE

For this recipe, you will need a total of ⅔ cup whole almonds, chopped or partially ground. For best results, lightly toast the almonds.

vanilla almond crust

18 vanilla sandwich creme filled cookies, with fillings intact
5 tablespoons butter or margarine, melted
3 tablespoons almonds, chopped

Crush cookies to make crumbs. Place crumbs in a mixing bowl and add butter, mix well. Press crumb mixture evenly onto bottom of greased 9-inch cheesecake pan. Sprinkle almonds on top of crust. Set aside.

Have all ingredients at room temperature. Preheat oven to 350 degrees.

amaretto filling

24 ounces cream cheese
¾ cup sugar
3 tablespoons cornstarch
3 large eggs
1 egg yolk
½ cup Amaretto
2 teaspoons almond extract
½ teaspoon lemon extract
1 teaspoon orange extract
⅓ cup almonds, toasted and chopped

In a large bowl, beat cream cheese, sugar, and cornstarch with an electric mixer until smooth. Add eggs and yolk one at a time, beating well after each addition. Stir in Amaretto and almond, lemon, and orange extracts. Stir until well blended. Stir in almonds. Pour filling onto crust. Bake at 350 degrees for 15 minutes.

i ♥ cheesecake

REDUCE HEAT TO 200 DEGREES and bake for 2 hours, or until center is firm and no longer looks wet or shiny. Remove cake from oven and carefully run a knife around inside edge of pan. Turn oven off and return cake to it for an additional 2 hours. Chill overnight.

chocolate whipped cream topping

1 cup semisweet chocolate chips

1 cup whipping cream

½ cup powdered sugar

1¼ teaspoons almond extract

2½ tablespoons almonds, chopped

Combine chocolate chips, whipping cream, powdered sugar, and almond extract in a heavy saucepan, stirring constantly over low heat until melted and smooth. Sprinkle chopped almonds over each slice to be served and serve with some warm sauce on top. Keep chilled.

AMARETTO CHOCOLATE CHEESECAKE

Impress your friends by serving this rich cheesecake at the next dinner party.

chocolate cookie crust

18 chocolate sandwich creme filled cookies, with fillings intact
5 tablespoons butter or margarine, melted

Crush cookies to make crumbs. Place crumbs in a mixing bowl and add butter, mix well. Press crumb mixture evenly onto bottom of greased 9-inch cheesecake pan. Set aside.

Have all ingredients at room temperature. Preheat oven to 350 degrees.

amaretto chocolate filling

32 ounces cream cheese
1 cup sugar
3 tablespoons cornstarch
4 tablespoons sour cream
4 large eggs
2 teaspoons vanilla extract
2 tablespoons cocoa
3 tablespoons sugar
3 ounces Amaretto
2 teaspoons almond extract
1 teaspoon lemon extract
⅓ cup almonds, chopped

In a large bowl, beat cream cheese, sugar, cornstarch, and sour cream with an electric mixer until smooth. Add eggs one at a time, beating well after each addition. Stir in vanilla extract. Remove 1 cup of mixture and put into a small bowl. Stir into this mixture cocoa and sugar. Set aside. Stir into original mixture Amaretto, almond and lemon extracts, and almonds. Pour half of original mixture onto crust. Spoon on 1 cup of cocoa mixture; spread this out making this the second layer. Pour the rest of original mixture on top of cocoa mixture; spread this out also. Spoon on rest of cocoa mixture. Without disturbing the crust, swirl a knife handle through cake, creating a marbling effect. Bake at 350 degrees for 15 minutes.

REDUCE HEAT TO 200 DEGREES and bake for 2 hours, or until center is firm and no longer looks wet or shiny. Remove cake from oven and run a knife around inside edge of pan. Turn oven off and return cake to it for an additional 2 hours. Chill overnight.

chocolate almond whipped cream topping

⅔ cup whipping cream
¼ cup powdered sugar
1 tablespoon cocoa
1 teaspoon almond extract
3 tablespoons almonds, chopped

Beat cream until it starts to thicken then add powdered sugar, cocoa, and almond extract. Beat until stiff. Spread topping on cake. Sprinkle almonds on top. Keep chilled.

AMARETTO WHITE CHOCOLATE CHEESECAKE

chocolate cookie crust

18 chocolate sandwich creme filled cookies, with fillings intact
5 tablespoons butter or margarine, softened

Crush cookies to make fine crumbs. Place crumbs in a mixing bowl and add butter, mix well. Press crumb mixture evenly onto bottom of greased 9-inch cheesecake pan. Set aside.

Have all ingredients at room temperature. Preheat oven to 350 degrees.

amaretto chocolate filling

32 ounces cream cheese
¾ cup sugar
3 tablespoons cornstarch
4 large eggs
½ cup Amaretto
¼ cup sour cream
8 ounces white chocolate, melted
2 teaspoons almond extract
2 teaspoons orange extract

In a large bowl, beat cream cheese, sugar, and cornstarch with an electric mixer until smooth. Add eggs one at a time, beating well after each addition. Stir in Amaretto, sour cream, and melted white chocolate and continue stirring until smooth. Stir in almond and orange extracts and continue stirring until well blended. Bake at 350 degrees for 15 minutes

REDUCE HEAT TO 200 DEGREES and bake for 2 hours, or until center is firm and no longer looks wet or shiny. Remove cake from oven and carefully run a knife around inside edge of pan. Turn oven off and return cake to it for an additional 2 hours. Chill overnight.

cream with marmalade topping

¾ cup heavy cream
2 teaspoons orange extract
2 envelopes whipped topping mix
¼ cup orange marmalade
almonds for decoration, toasted, whole or chopped
½ cup maraschino cherries, pitted and halved

In a medium bowl, beat cream, orange extract, and whipped topping mix with an electric mixer until thickened and stiff. Carefully blend in orange marmalade and continue stirring until evenly mixed. Spread topping over cake and place almonds and cherries on top, creating a design. Keep chilled.

CHOCOLATE IRISH CREAM CHEESECAKE

mocha cookie crust

18 chocolate sandwich creme filled cookies, with fillings intact
2 teaspoons instant coffee, dissolved in 2 teaspoons boiling water
5 tablespoons butter or margarine, melted

Crush cookies to make crumbs. Place crumbs in a mixing bowl and add dissolved coffee and butter, mix well. Press crumb mixture evenly onto bottom of greased 9-inch cheesecake pan. Set aside.

Have all ingredients at room temperature. Preheat oven to 350 degrees.

chocolate irish cream filling

24 ounces cream cheese
¾ cup sugar
3 tablespoons cornstarch
4 large eggs
½ cup whipping cream
½ cup Irish cream liqueur
2 teaspoons vanilla extract
2 teaspoons instant coffee, dissolved in 2 teaspoons boiling water
12 ounces milk chocolate chips, melted

In a large bowl, beat cream cheese, sugar, and cornstarch with an electric mixer until smooth. Add eggs one at a time, beating well after each addition. Stir in cream, Irish cream liqueur, vanilla extract, and coffee. Add melted chocolate and gently, but thoroughly, mix together. Pour filling onto crust. Bake at 350 degrees for 15 minutes.

REDUCE HEAT TO 200 DEGREES and bake for 2 hours, or until center is firm and no longer looks wet or shiny. Remove cake from oven and carefully run a knife around inside edge of pan. Turn oven off and return cake to it for an additional 2 hours. Chill overnight.

powdered sugar topping

Place a decorative stencil over the top of the cheesecake. Sift powdered sugar over the stencil. Carefully remove stencil. Chill until serving time.

COFFEE 'N CREAM CHEESECAKE

vanilla wafer crust

2 cups vanilla wafers, crushed
2 teaspoons instant coffee, dissolved in 2 teaspoons boiling water
5 tablespoons butter or margarine, melted
3 tablespoons sugar
¼ cup almonds, toasted and chopped

Place vanilla wafer crumbs in medium mixing bowl, add dissolved coffee and melted butter, mix well. Add sugar, mix well. Press crumb mixture evenly onto bottom of greased 9-inch cheesecake pan. Sprinkle almonds on top of crust. Set aside.

Have all ingredients at room temperature. Preheat oven to 350 degrees.

coffee filling

32 ounces cream cheese
3 tablespoons cornstarch
1 cup sugar
4 large eggs
2 rounded teaspoons instant coffee, dissolved in 2 teaspoons boiling water
2 teaspoons vanilla extract
1¼ teaspoons almond extract
¾ cup whipping cream

Note: For a stronger coffee flavor, substitute coffee liqueur for cream and substitute 2 teaspoons of instant coffee dissolved in 2 teaspoons of boiling water for 2 rounded teaspoons of instant coffee.

i ♥ cheesecake

In a large bowl, beat cream cheese, cornstarch, and sugar with an electric mixer until smooth. Add eggs one at a time, beating well after each addition. Stir in coffee and vanilla and almond extracts. Add cream, mix well. Pour filling onto crust. Bake at 350 degrees for 15 minutes.

REDUCE HEAT TO 200 DEGREES and bake for 2 hours, or until center is firm and no longer looks wet or shiny. Remove cake from oven and carefully run a knife around inside edge of pan. Turn oven off and return cake to it for an additional 2 hours. Chill overnight.

mocha whipped cream topping

¾ cup whipping cream
¼ cup powdered sugar
2 teaspoons instant coffee, dissolved in 2 teaspoons boiling water
3 tablespoons almonds, toasted and chopped

In a bowl, beat cream, powdered sugar, and coffee mixture until stiff. Spread over cake. Decorate with chopped almonds. Keep chilled.

DAIQUIRI CHEESECAKE

Pucker up for this lime-flavored cheesecake.

graham cracker crust

2 cups graham crumbs

5 tablespoons butter or margarine

3 tablespoons sugar

Place crumbs in a mixing bowl and add butter and sugar, mix well. Press crumb mixture evenly onto bottom of greased 9-inch cheesecake pan. Set aside.

Have all ingredients at room temperature. Preheat oven to 350 degrees.

daiquiri filling

32 ounces cream cheese

1 cup sugar

3 tablespoons cornstarch

4 large eggs

6 ounces frozen concentrated limeade, thawed

2 tablespoons light rum

2 drops green food coloring

In a large bowl, beat cream cheese, sugar, and cornstarch with an electric mixer until smooth. Add eggs one at a time, beating well after each addition. Stir in limeade, rum, and food coloring. Pour filling onto crust. Bake at 350 degrees for 15 minutes.

REDUCE HEAT TO 200 DEGREES and bake for 2 hours, or until center is firm and no longer looks wet or shiny. Remove cake from oven and carefully run a knife around inside edge of pan. Turn oven off and return cake to it for an additional 2 hours. Chill overnight.

i ♥ cheesecake

lime glaze

½ cup frozen concentrated limeade, thawed
4 teaspoons cornstarch
4 teaspoons sugar
1 tablespoon light rum
Grated zest of ½ lime for decoration

In a small heavy saucepan, stir together limeade, cornstarch, sugar, and rum. Cook and stir over low heat until thickened and bubbly—about 2 minutes. Pour this over cake while topping is still hot. Sprinkle lime zest on top. Keep chilled.

Note: Grate the outer lime peel to make zest.

EGGNOG CHEESECAKE

If you want to leave the rum out of this holiday flavored cake, simply increase the whipping cream to ⅓ cup.

chocolate cookie crust

18 chocolate sandwich creme filled cookies, with fillings intact
⅛ teaspoon nutmeg
5 tablespoons butter or margarine, melted

Crush cookies to make crumbs. Place crumbs in a mixing bowl and add nutmeg and butter, mix well. Press crumb mixture evenly onto bottom of greased 9-inch cheesecake pan. Set aside.

Have all ingredients at room temperature. Preheat oven to 350 degrees.

eggnog filling

32 ounces cream cheese
1 cup sugar
3 tablespoons cornstarch
4 large eggs
2 teaspoons vanilla extract
1½ teaspoons nutmeg
¼ cup whipping cream
2 tablespoons light rum

In a large bowl, beat cream cheese, sugar, and cornstarch with an electric mixer until smooth. Add eggs one at a time, beating well after each addition. Stir in vanilla extract, nutmeg, cream, and rum, mix well. Pour filling onto crust. Bake at 350 degrees for 15 minutes.

REDUCE HEAT TO 200 DEGREES and bake for 2 hours, or until center is firm and no longer looks wet or shiny. Remove cake from oven and carefully run a knife around inside edge of pan. Turn oven off and return cake to it for an additional 2 hours. Chill overnight.

i ♥ cheesecake

whipped cream topping with nutmeg

⅔ cup whipping cream
3 tablespoons powdered sugar
½ teaspoon vanilla extract
⅛ teaspoon nutmeg

In a bowl, beat cream and powdered sugar until it starts to thicken. Add vanilla extract and nutmeg, beat until stiff. Spread over cake. Keep chilled.

GRANDE PASSION CHEESECAKE

This tropical cheesecake gets its great flavor from La Grande Passion Liqueur.

Preheat oven to 350 degrees.

coconut crust

2 cups coconut, flaked or freshly grated
4 tablespoons butter or margarine, melted

Place coconut in a mixing bowl and add butter, mix well. Press coconut mixture evenly onto bottom of greased 9-inch cheesecake pan. Bake 12–15 minutes or until golden. Set aside.

Have all ingredients at room temperature. Keep oven at 350 degrees.

la grande passion and pineapple filling

32 ounces cream cheese
1 cup sugar
3 tablespoons cornstarch
4 large eggs
½ cup La Grande Passion
2 teaspoons vanilla extract
1½ teaspoons lemon extract
⅔ cup crushed pineapple, well drained

In a large bowl, beat cream cheese, sugar, and cornstarch with an electric mixer until smooth. Add eggs one at a time, beating well after each addition. Stir in the La Grande Passion and vanilla and lemon extracts. Stir in crushed pineapple. Pour filling onto crust. Without disturbing crust, swirl the handle of a knife through the filling to distribute pineapple evenly. Bake at 350 degrees for 15 minutes.

i ♥ cheesecake

REDUCE HEAT TO 200 DEGREES and bake for 2 hours, or until center no longer looks wet or shiny. Remove cake from oven and run a knife around inside edge of pan. Turn oven off and return cake to it for an additional 2 hours. Chill overnight.

tropical fruit topping

¾ cup pineapple preserves
¼ cup frozen concentrated tropical citrus beverage, thawed
2 tablespoons La Grande Passion
2 teaspoons cornstarch
2 tablespoons crushed pineapple, well drained
2 tablespoons almonds, chopped
½ kiwi, peeled and sliced

In a small heavy saucepan, combine preserves, tropical beverage, La Grande Passion, and cornstarch. Stir constantly over low heat until thickened. Spread warm topping on cake. Decorate top with crushed pineapple, almonds, and sliced kiwi. Keep chilled.

GRASSHOPPER CHEESECAKE

This minty dessert tastes as good as the thick, frosty after-dinner drink that goes by the same name.

Make a chocolate cookie crust either with chocolate mint sandwich creme filled cookies or with chocolate sandwich creme filled cookies.

chocolate cookie crust

18 sandwich cookies, with fillings intact
5 tablespoons butter or margarine, melted

Crush cookies to make crumbs. Place crumbs in a mixing bowl and add butter, mix well. Press crumb mixture evenly onto bottom of greased 9-inch cheesecake pan. Set aside.

Have all ingredients at room temperature. Preheat oven to 350 degrees.

crème de menthe filling

32 ounces cream cheese
1 cup sugar
3 tablespoons cornstarch
4 large eggs
2 teaspoons vanilla extract
½ cup crème de menthe
2 drops green food coloring

In a large bowl, beat cream cheese, sugar, and cornstarch with an electric mixer until smooth. Add eggs one at a time, beating well after each addition. Stir in vanilla extract, crème de menthe, and green food coloring. Pour filling onto crust. Bake at 350 degrees for 15 minutes.

REDUCE HEAT TO 200 DEGREES and bake for 2 hours, or until center no longer looks wet or shiny. Remove cake from oven and run a knife around inside edge of pan. Turn oven off and return to oven for an additional 2 hours. Chill overnight.

chocolate glaze

½ cup semisweet chocolate chips
1 tablespoon shortening or butter
shaved white chocolate

In a small heavy saucepan, melt chocolate and shortening over low heat, stirring constantly. Spread warm chocolate mixture over cheesecake. Garnish with shaved white chocolate. Chill until serving time.

HAWAIIAN TROPICAL BLEND CHEESECAKE

Preheat oven to 350 degrees.

coconut crust

2 cups coconut, flaked or freshly grated
1 tablespoon almonds, coarsely chopped
4 tablespoons butter or margarine, softened

Place coconut and almonds in a mixing bowl and add butter, mix well. Press mixture evenly onto bottom of greased 9-inch cheesecake pan. Bake 12–15 minutes or until golden. Set aside.

Have all ingredients at room temperature. Keep oven at 350 degrees.

fruit flavored filling

32 ounces cream cheese
1 cup sugar
3 tablespoons cornstarch
4 large eggs
⅓ cup frozen concentrated tropical fruit flavored juice, thawed
¼ cup tropical fruit schnapps
2 teaspoons vanilla extract
1 teaspoon almond extract
¼ cup crushed pineapple, well drained

In a large bowl, beat cream cheese, sugar, and cornstarch with an electric mixer until smooth. Add eggs one at a time, beating well after each addition. Add tropical fruit juice, fruit schnapps, and vanilla and almond extracts, mix well. Stir in crushed pineapple. Pour filling onto crust. Without disturbing the crust, swirl the handle of a knife through the filling to distribute the pineapple evenly. Bake at 350 degrees for 15 minutes.

REDUCE HEAT TO 200 DEGREES and bake for 2 hours, or until center no longer looks wet or shiny. Remove cake from oven and carefully run a knife around inside edge of pan. Turn oven off and return cake to it for as additional 2 hours. Chill overnight.

tropical fruit topping

sliced star fruit
sliced mango
sliced papaya
1 cup orange marmalade

Before serving, arrange fresh fruit over cheesecake. Heat marmalade in small heavy saucepan over low heat, stirring constantly. Drizzle over cheesecake and serve.

IRISH CREAM CHEESECAKE

Yes, it's as sumptuous as it sounds!

mocha cookie crust

18 chocolate sandwich creme filled cookies, with fillings intact
2 teaspoons instant coffee, dissolved in 2 teaspoons boiling water
5 tablespoons butter or margarine, melted

Crush cookies to make crumbs. Place crumbs in a mixing bowl and add coffee and butter, mix well. Press crumb mixture evenly onto bottom of greased 9-inch cheesecake pan. Set aside.

Have all ingredients at room temperature. Preheat oven to 350 degrees.

coffee liqueur filling

32 ounces cream cheese
1 cup sugar
3 tablespoons cornstarch
3 tablespoons cocoa
4 large eggs
⅔ cup Irish cream liqueur
2 teaspoons vanilla extract
2 teaspoons instant coffee, dissolved in 2 teaspoons boiling water

In a large bowl, beat cream cheese, sugar, cornstarch, and cocoa with an electric mixer until smooth. Add eggs one at a time, beating well after each addition. Stir in Irish cream liqueur, vanilla extract, and dissolved coffee. Pour filling onto crust. Bake at 350 degrees for 15 minutes.

REDUCE HEAT TO 200 DEGREES and bake for 2 hours, or until center no longer looks wet or shiny. Remove cake from oven and carefully run a knife around inside edge of pan. Turn oven off and return cake to it for an additional 2 hours. Chill overnight.

mocha whipped cream topping

½ cup whipping cream
2 envelopes whipped topping mix
2 tablespoons powdered sugar
1 tablespoon cocoa
1 teaspoon instant coffee, dissolved in 1 teaspoon boiling water

In a bowl, combine cream, whipped topping mix, powdered sugar, and cocoa until well mixed. Add dissolved coffee and beat until stiff. Spread whipped cream over cake. Keep chilled.

JAMAICAN BANANA CHEESECAKE

You will discover fresh bananas, rum, and crème de cacao in this island cheesecake.

chocolate cookie crust

18 chocolate sandwich creme filled cookies, with fillings intact
5 tablespoons butter or margarine, melted

Crush cookies to make crumbs. Add butter, mix well. Press cookie mixture evenly onto bottom of greased 9-inch cheesecake pan. Set aside.

Have all ingredients at room temperature. Preheat oven to 350 degrees.

banana liqueur filling

32 ounces cream cheese
1 cup sugar
3 tablespoons cornstarch
½ cup pureed bananas (1 small banana)
4 large eggs
2 tablespoons banana schnapps
2 tablespoons crème de cacao, white
2 tablespoons light rum
2 teaspoons vanilla extract

In a large bowl, beat cream cheese, sugar, cornstarch, and bananas with electric mixer until smooth. Add eggs one at a time, beating well after each addition. Stir in banana schnapps, crème de cacao, and rum. Stir in vanilla extract. Pour filling onto crust. Bake at 350 degrees for 15 minutes.

REDUCE HEAT TO 200 DEGREES and bake for 2 hours, or until center no longer looks wet or shiny. Remove cake from oven and run a knife around inside edge of pan. Turn oven off and return cake to it for an additional 2 hours. Chill overnight.

i ♥ cheesecake

fresh fruit topping

fresh fruit, sliced
chocolate ice cream topping (the type that forms a hardened shell)

Arrange fresh fruit over cheesecake. Drizzle with chocolate topping. Keep chilled.

MAI TAI CHEESECAKE

Makes 12–18 slices

You will find the fruity flavors of the classic Mai Tai cocktail in this rich and creamy cheesecake.

Preheat oven to 350 degrees.

coconut crust

2 cups coconut, flaked or freshly grated
4 tablespoons butter or margarine, melted

Place coconut in a mixing bowl and add butter, mix well. Press coconut mixture evenly onto bottom of greased 9-inch cheesecake pan. Bake 12–15 minutes or until golden. Set aside.

Have all ingredients at room temperature. Keep oven at 350 degrees.

orange liqueur filling

32 ounces cream cheese
1 cup sugar
3 tablespoons cornstarch
4 large eggs
¼ cup frozen concentrated orange juice, thawed
½ teaspoon almond extract
2 tablespoons grenadine syrup
¼ cup triple sec, liqueur
¼ cup light rum

In a large bowl, beat cream cheese, sugar, and cornstarch with an electric mixer until smooth. Add eggs one at a time, beating well after each addition. Stir in orange juice, almond extract, grenadine syrup, triple sec, and rum. Pour filling onto crust. Bake at 350 degrees for 15 minutes.

i ♥ cheesecake

REDUCE HEAT TO 200 DEGREES and bake for 2 hours, or until center no longer looks wet or shiny. Remove cake from oven and run a knife around inside edge of pan. Turn oven off and return cake to it for an additional 2 hours. Chill overnight.

orange glaze

½ cup frozen concentrated orange juice, thawed
1 tablespoon lime juice
1 tablespoon grenadine syrup
2 teaspoons cornstarch
1 tablespoon triple sec, liqueur
1 tablespoon light rum
fresh fruit, sliced

In a small heavy saucepan, stir together orange juice concentrate, lime juice, grenadine syrup, and cornstarch. Cook and stir until thickened and bubbly. Cook 2 minutes more. Stir in triple sec and rum. Pour over cheesecake and garnish with fruit. Keep chilled.

MARBLED GRASSHOPPER CHEESECAKE

Rich chocolate cheesecake is swirled through creamy crème de menthe cheesecake to create a sensational combination.

Make a chocolate cookie crust either with chocolate mint sandwich creme filled cookies or with chocolate sandwich creme filled cookies.

chocolate cookie crust

18 sandwich cookies, with fillings intact
5 tablespoons butter or margarine, melted

Crush cookies to make crumbs. Place crumbs in a mixing bowl and add butter, mix well. Press crumb mixture evenly onto bottom of greased 9-inch cheesecake pan. Set aside.

Have all ingredients at room temperature. Preheat oven to 350 degrees.

chocolate mint filling

32 ounces cream cheese
1 cup sugar
4 large eggs
¼ cup sour cream
½ teaspoon lemon extract
2 tablespoons cornstarch
2 tablespoons cocoa
3 tablespoons sugar
¼ cup crème de menthe
a few drops green food coloring

In a large bowl, beat cream cheese and 1 cup sugar with an electric mixer until smooth. Add eggs one at a time, beating well after each addition. Stir in sour cream, lemon extract, and cornstarch. Remove

i ♥ cheesecake

1 cup of mixture and put in a small bowl. Stir in to this mixture the cocoa and 3 tablespoons sugar. Set aside. Stir into the original mixture the crème de menthe and food coloring. Pour half of the original mixture onto the crust. Spoon on half of the cocoa mixture. Pour remaining original mixture on top of cocoa mixture. Spoon on the rest of the cocoa mixture. Without disturbing the crust, swirl the handle of a knife through the cake, creating a marbling effect. Bake at 350 degrees for 15 minutes.

REDUCE HEAT TO 200 DEGREES and bake for 2 hours, or until center no longer looks wet or shiny. Remove cake from oven and run a knife around inside edge of pan. Turn oven off and return cake to it for an additional 2 hours. Chill overnight.

chocolate sour cream topping

5 ounces chocolate chips
⅓ cup sour cream
1 tablespoon crème de menthe
1 tablespoon sugar

Place all ingredients in a small heavy saucepan. Stir constantly over low heat until melted and smooth. Spread warm topping on cake. Keep chilled.

MARGARITA CHEESECAKE

This tequila-flavored cheesecake tastes like the popular drink it's named after, minus the salt.

Preheat oven to 350 degrees.

homemade cookie crust

¾ cup flour
2 tablespoons sugar
1 egg, lightly beaten
¼ cup butter or margarine, softened
¾ teaspoon vanilla extract

Mix flour and sugar. Add egg then butter and vanilla extract. Mix well. With generously greased fingers, press dough evenly onto bottom of greased 9-inch cheesecake pan. Bake 12–15 minutes, until lightly browned. Remove from oven and set aside.

Have all ingredients at room temperature. Keep oven at 350 degrees.

lime filling

32 ounces cream cheese
1 cup sugar
3 tablespoons cornstarch
4 large eggs
1¼ teaspoons lemon extract
3 tablespoons light tequila
½ cup triple sec
½ cup frozen concentrated limeade, thawed

In a large bowl, beat cream cheese, sugar, and cornstarch with an electric mixer until smooth. Add eggs one at a time, beating well after each addition. Add lemon extract. Stir in tequila, triple sec, and limeade. Pour filling onto crust. Bake at 350 degrees for 15 minutes.

i ♥ cheesecake

REDUCE HEAT TO 200 DEGREES and bake for 2 hours, or until center no longer looks wet or shiny. Remove cake from oven and carefully run a knife around inside edge of pan. Turn oven off and return cake to it for an additional 2 hours. Chill overnight.

lime glaze

½ cup frozen concentrated limeade, thawed
2 teaspoons cornstarch
1 tablespoon triple sec
1 teaspoon tequila
½ teaspoon orange extract
fresh lime wedges

In a small heavy saucepan, stir together limeade and cornstarch. Stir in triple sec, tequila, and orange extract. Cook and stir over low heat until thickened and bubbly. Spread warm topping on cake. Garnish with lime. Keep chilled.

MOCHA CHEESECAKE

mocha cookie crust

18 chocolate sandwich creme filled cookies, with fillings intact
2 teaspoons instant coffee, dissolved in 2 teaspoons boiling water
5 tablespoons of butter or margarine, melted

This is a classic chocolate and coffee combination.

Crush cookies to make crumbs. Place crumbs in a mixing bowl, add dissolved coffee and butter, mix well. Press crumb mixture evenly onto bottom of greased 9-inch cheesecake pan.

Have all ingredients at room temperature. Preheat oven to 350 degrees.

mocha filling

32 ounces cream cheese
1 cup sugar
3 tablespoons cornstarch
½ cup sour cream
1 tablespoon instant coffee, dissolved in 1 tablespoon boiling water
2 teaspoons vanilla extract
4 large eggs
8 ounces semisweet chocolate chips, melted

In a large bowl, beat cream cheese, sugar, and cornstarch with an electric mixer until smooth. Stir in sour cream, coffee, and vanilla extract. Add eggs one at a time, beating well after each addition. Add melted chocolate, mix well. Pour filling onto crust. Bake at 350 degrees for 15 minutes.

REDUCE HEAT TO 200 DEGREES and bake for 2 hours, or until center no longer looks wet or shiny. Remove cake from oven and carefully run a knife around inside edge of pan. Turn oven off and return cake to it for an additional 2 hours. Chill overnight.

i ♥ cheesecake

mocha glaze

5 ounces semisweet chocolate chips
¼ cup sour cream
1 teaspoon instant coffee, dissolved in 1 teaspoon boiling water
3 tablespoons pecans, walnuts, or almonds, chopped

Place chocolate chips and sour cream in a small heavy saucepan. Melt chocolate over low heat, stirring constantly. Stir in dissolved coffee. Spread glaze over cake. Decorate with chopped nuts. Keep chilled.

NEAPOLITAN ROYALE CHEESECAKE

This is a sophisticated combination of chocolate, vanilla, and strawberry cheesecake.

chocolate cookie crust

18 chocolate sandwich creme filled cookies, with fillings intact
5 tablespoons butter or margarine, melted

Crush cookies to make crumbs. Place crumbs in a mixing bowl and add butter, mix well. Press crumb mixture evenly onto bottom of greased 9-inch cheesecake pan. Set aside.

Have all ingredients at room temperature. Preheat oven to 350 degrees.

chocolate, strawberry, and vanilla filling

32 ounces cream cheese
1 cup sugar
3 tablespoons cornstarch
4 large eggs
3 tablespoons strawberry schnapps or strawberry flavoring
2 drops of red food coloring
½ cup sour cream
2 tablespoons vanilla extract
¼ cup crème de cacao
2 tablespoons cocoa
3 tablespoons sugar

In a large bowl, beat cream cheese, 1 cup sugar, and cornstarch with an electric mixer until smooth. Add eggs one at a time, beating well after each addition. Remove 1 cup of mixture and put into a small bowl. To this mixture, add strawberry schnapps and food coloring. Mix thoroughly and set aside. Remove another 1 cup of mixture and put into another small bowl. To this mixture, add sour cream and vanilla extract, mix thoroughly. Set aside. To the original mixture, add crème de cacao, cocoa, and 3 tablespoons sugar, mix well. Pour the chocolate mixture onto the crust. Spoon on the strawberry mixture carefully, spreading it out to make the second layer. Spoon on the vanilla mixture and carefully spread it out. Bake at 350 degrees for 15 minutes.

REDUCE HEAT TO 200 DEGREES and bake for 2 hours, or until center no longer looks wet or shiny. Remove cake from oven and run a knife around inside edge of pan. Turn oven off and return cake to it for an additional 2 hours. Chill overnight.

whipped cream topping

½ cup whipping cream
2 envelopes whipped topping mix
12–18 strawberries, with stems removed
chocolate ice cream topping (the type that forms a hardened shell)

In a small bowl, beat cream and whipped topping mix with an electric mixer until fluffy. Either cover the top of the cake with the whipped cream or pipe the cream around the edge of the top of the cheesecake. Place the strawberries on a plate and squeeze some chocolate topping on the top portion of each berry. Refrigerate berries until chocolate hardens. Transfer berries to top of cheesecake. Keep chilled.

NUTTY COLADA CHEESECAKE

Preheat oven to 350 degrees.

coconut crust

2 cups coconut, flaked or freshly grated
3 tablespoons almonds, toasted and coarsely chopped
4 tablespoons butter or margarine, melted

Place coconut and almonds in a mixing bowl and add butter, mix well. Press mixture evenly onto bottom of greased 9-inch cheesecake pan. Sprinkle almonds on top. Bake 12–15 minutes or until golden. Set aside.

Have all ingredients at room temperature. Keep oven at 350 degrees.

coconut, almond, and pineapple filling

32 ounces cream cheese
1 cup sugar
3 tablespoons cornstarch
4 large eggs
⅓ cup cream of coconut
⅓ cup Amaretto
2 teaspoons vanilla extract
1¼ teaspoons almond extract
2 teaspoons pineapple extract
⅓ cup crushed pineapple, well drained
½ cup almonds, toasted and coarsely chopped

For a fresher taste and a crunchier texture, use fresh coconut and toasted almonds.

i ♥ cheesecake

In a large bowl, beat cream cheese, sugar, and cornstarch with an electric mixer until smooth. Add eggs one at a time, beating well after each addition. Stir in cream of coconut, Amaretto, and vanilla, almond, and pineapple extracts. Stir in crushed pineapple and almonds. Pour filling onto crust. Without disturbing the crust, swirl the handle of a knife through the batter to distribute the pineapple and almonds evenly. Bake at 350 degrees for 15 minutes.

REDUCE HEAT TO 200 DEGREES and bake for 2 hours, or until center no longer looks wet or shiny. Remove cake from oven and run a knife around inside edge of pan. Turn oven off and return cake to it for an additional 2 hours. Chill overnight.

coconut, almond, and pineapple topping

½ cup whipping cream
2 envelopes of whipped topping mix
½ teaspoon almond extract
2 tablespoons coconut, flaked or freshly grated
2 tablespoons crushed pineapple, well drained
3 tablespoons almonds, toasted and coarsely chopped

In a small bowl, combine cream and whipped topping mix. Add almond extract and beat until thickened. Spread whipped cream over cake. Sprinkle coconut, pineapple, and almonds on top. Keep chilled.

ORANGE PINEAPPLE ALOHA CHEESECAKE

Preheat oven to 350 degrees.

coconut crust

2 cups coconut, flaked or freshly grated
4 tablespoons butter or margarine, melted

If pineapple orange juice concentrate is unavailable, use frozen orange juice concentrate and 1 teaspoon pineapple flavoring.

Place coconut in a mixing bowl and add butter, mix well. Press coconut mixture evenly onto bottom of greased 9-inch cheesecake pan. Bake 12–15 minutes or until golden. Set aside.

Have all ingredients at room temperature. Keep oven at 350 degrees.

orange pineapple filling

32 ounces cream cheese
1 cup sugar
3 tablespoons cornstarch
4 large eggs
2 teaspoons vanilla extract
2 teaspoons orange extract
2 teaspoons pineapple flavoring
2 tablespoons rum
½ cup triple sec
½ cup frozen concentrated pineapple orange juice, thawed

In a large bowl, beat cream cheese, sugar, and cornstarch with an electric mixer until smooth. Add eggs one at a time, beating well after each addition. Stir in vanilla and orange extracts, and pineapple flavoring. Stir in rum, triple sec, and pineapple orange juice. Pour filling onto crust. Bake at 350 degrees for 15 minutes.

i ♥ cheesecake

REDUCE HEAT TO 200 DEGREES and bake for 2 hours, or until center no longer looks wet or shiny. Remove cake from oven and run a knife around inside edge of pan. Turn oven off and return cake to it for an additional 2 hours. Chill overnight.

orange pineapple glaze

¾ cup orange marmalade

¼ cup frozen concentrated pineapple orange juice, thawed

2 tablespoons triple sec

2 teaspoons cornstarch

2 tablespoons coconut, flaked or freshly grated

In a small heavy saucepan, stir together the marmalade, pineapple orange juice, triple sec, and cornstarch. Cook over low heat, stirring constantly, for about 5 minutes until thickened. Remove from heat and spread topping over the cake. Sprinkle coconut on top. Keep chilled.

PEACHY ORANGE CHEESECAKE

Preheat oven to 350 degrees. Use either a homemade cookie crust or a refrigerated slice-and-bake sugar cookie dough.

homemade cookie crust

¾ cup flour
2 tablespoons sugar
1 egg, lightly beaten
4 tablespoons butter or margarine, softened
½ teaspoon vanilla extract

Mix flour and sugar. Add egg, butter, and vanilla extract, mix well. With generously greased fingers, press dough evenly onto bottom of greased 9-inch cheesecake pan. Bake at 350 degrees for 12–15 minutes or until lightly browned. Set aside.

slice-and-bake cookie crust

Use 8 ounces of a roll of slice-and-bake refrigerated sugar cookie dough. Slice as you would to make cookies. With generously greased fingers, arrange in circles, starting on the outside edge of the pan and working your way in, on the bottom of the pan. With fingertips, press dough evenly onto the bottom of the pan as if to make one big cookie. Bake 12–15 minutes, until lightly browned. Remove from oven and set aside.

Have all ingredients at room temperature. Keep oven at 350 degrees.

peachy orange filling

32 ounces cream cheese
1 cup sugar
3 tablespoons cornstarch

4 large eggs
2 teaspoons vanilla extract
1 tablespoon orange extract
½ cup frozen concentrated orange juice, thawed
1 cup peaches, peeled and sliced
2 drops orange food coloring

In a large bowl, beat cream cheese, sugar, and cornstarch with an electric mixer until smooth. Add eggs one at a time, beating well after each addition. Add vanilla and orange extracts. Stir in orange juice, peaches, and food coloring. Pour filling onto crust. Bake at 350 degrees for 15 minutes.

REDUCE HEAT TO 200 DEGREES and bake for 2 hours, or until center no longer looks wet or shiny. Remove cake from oven and carefully run a knife around inside edge of pan. Turn oven off and return cake to it for an additional 2 hours. Chill overnight.

orange marmalade topping

¾ cup orange marmalade
2 tablespoons orange juice concentrate, thawed
1 tablespoon cornstarch
2 teaspoons lemon juice

In a small heavy saucepan, stir together marmalade, orange juice, cornstarch, and lemon juice. Cook and stir over low heat until somewhat thickened—about 5 minutes. Remove from heat. Spread topping on cake while it is still warm. Keep chilled.

PINA COLADA CHEESECAKE

Make this refreshing cheesecake for your next pool party or beach party.

Preheat oven to 350 degrees.

homemade cookie crust

1 cup flour
¼ cup sugar
1 egg, lightly beaten
¼ cup butter or margarine, softened
1 teaspoon vanilla extract

Mix flour and sugar in a medium bowl. Add egg, then butter and vanilla extract, mix well. With generously greased fingertips, press dough evenly onto bottom of greased 9-inch cheesecake pan. Bake 12–15 minutes or until lightly browned. Remove from oven and set aside.

slice-and-bake cookie crust

Use 8 ounces of a roll of slice-and-bake refrigerated sugar cookie dough. Slice as you would to make cookies. With generously greased fingers, arrange in circles, starting on outside edge of pan and working your way in, on the bottom of the pan. With fingertips, press dough evenly onto bottom of the pan as if to make one big cookie.

Have all ingredients at room temperature. Keep oven at 350 degrees.

pineapple, rum, and coconut filling

32 ounces cream cheese
1 cup sugar
3 tablespoons cornstarch
4 large eggs
2 teaspoons pineapple extract

i ♥ cheesecake

2 teaspoons rum extract
¼ cup cream of coconut
¼ cup frozen concentrated pineapple juice, thawed
¼ cup light rum
8 ounces can crushed pineapple, well drained
⅓ cup grated coconut

In a large bowl, beat cream cheese, sugar, and cornstarch with an electric mixer until smooth. Add eggs one at a time, beating well after each addition. Stir in pineapple and rum extracts. Blend in cream of coconut and pineapple juice. Stir in rum, crushed pineapple, and grated coconut. Pour filling onto crust. Bake at 350 degrees for 15 minutes.

REDUCE HEAT TO 200 DEGREES and bake for 2 hours, or until center no longer looks wet or shiny. Remove cake from oven and run a knife around inside edge of pan. Turn oven off and return cake to it for an additional 2 hours. Chill overnight.

pineapple, rum, and coconut topping

½ cup whipping cream
2 envelopes whipped topping mix
1 tablespoon light rum
¼ cup grated coconut
fresh pineapple sliced, for decoration
maraschino cherries, for decoration

In a medium bowl, beat cream, whipped topping mix, and rum until stiff. Stir in coconut, blending well. Spread topping over cake. Decorate with pineapple and cherries. Keep chilled.

PINK LEMONADE CHEESECAKE

lemon cookie crust

18 lemon sandwich creme filled cookies, with fillings intact
5 tablespoons butter or margarine, melted

Crush cookies to make crumbs. Put crumbs in mixing bowl and add butter, mix well. Press crumb mixture evenly onto bottom of greased 9-inch cheesecake pan. Set aside.

Have all ingredients at room temperature. Preheat oven to 350 degrees.

lemonade filling

32 ounces cream cheese
1 cup sugar
3 tablespoons cornstarch
4 large eggs
6 ounces frozen concentrated pink lemonade, thawed (if pink is not available, use regular)
2 teaspoons lemon extract
1 drop of red food coloring

In large bowl, beat cream cheese, sugar, and cornstarch with an electric mixer until smooth. Add eggs one at a time, beating well after each addition. Stir in lemonade, lemon extract, and food coloring. Pour filling onto crust. Bake at 350 degrees for 15 minutes.

REDUCE HEAT TO 200 DEGREES and bake for 2 hours, or until center no longer looks wet or shiny. Remove cake from oven and run a knife around inside edge of pan. Turn oven off and return cake to it for an additional 2 hours. Chill overnight.

i ♥ cheesecake

5 ounces white chocolate
¼ cup sour cream
1 teaspoon lemon extract
lemon slices

In small heavy saucepan, combine white chocolate, sour cream, and lemon extract and melt over low heat, stirring constantly. Spread hot topping over cake. Decorate with lemon slices, if desired. Keep chilled.

RUM RAISIN CHEESECAKE

This cheesecake tastes like rum raisin ice cream.

vanilla cookie crust

2 cups vanilla wafers, crushed

3 tablespoons golden raisins

5 tablespoons butter or margarine, melted

Place crumbs and raisins in a mixing bowl, add butter, and mix well. Press crumb mixture evenly onto bottom of greased 9-inch cheesecake pan. Set aside.

Have all ingredients at room temperature. Preheat oven to 350 degrees.

rum raisin filling

⅔ cup golden raisins soaked in ¼ cup light rum

32 ounces cream cheese

1 cup sugar

½ cup whipping cream

3 tablespoons cornstarch

4 large eggs

1 egg yolk

1 tablespoon vanilla extract

½ cup vanilla-flavored liqueur

In a small bowl, soak raisins in rum for 1 hour, drain reserve rum. If necessary, add more rum to measure 2 tablespoons. In a large bowl, combine cream cheese, sugar, cream, and cornstarch with an electric mixer until smooth. Add eggs and yolk one at a time, beating well after each addition. Stir in raisins, reserved rum, vanilla extract, and liqueur, mix well. Pour filling onto crust. Bake at 350 degrees for 15 minutes.

i ♥ cheesecake

REDUCE HEAT TO 200 DEGREES and bake for 2 hours, or until center no longer looks wet or shiny. Remove cake from oven and carefully run a knife around inside edge of pan. Turn oven off and return cake to it for an additional 2 hours. Chill overnight.

rum raisin white chocolate topping

3 tablespoons golden raisins
2 teaspoons light rum
6 ounces white chocolate
¼ cup sour cream
1 teaspoon vanilla extract

In a small bowl, soak raisins in rum for 30 minutes. Place white chocolate and sour cream in a small heavy saucepan and melt over low heat, stirring constantly, until melted and smooth. Stir in vanilla extract. Spread chocolate mixture over cake. Sprinkle with raisins. Keep chilled.

STRAWBERRY SMOOTHIE CHEESECAKE

Make this when fresh strawberries are in season!

graham cracker crust

2 cups graham cracker crumbs
5 tablespoons butter or margarine, melted
3 tablespoons sugar

Place crumbs in a mixing bowl, add butter and sugar, mix well. Press crumb mixture evenly onto bottom of greased 9-inch cheesecake pan. Set aside.

Have all ingredients at room temperature. Preheat oven to 350 degrees.

strawberry filling

32 ounces cream cheese
1 cup sugar
3 tablespoons cornstarch
4 large eggs
1 tablespoon lemon juice
2 teaspoons vanilla extract
2 drops red food coloring
1¼ cups fresh strawberries, washed, hulled, and sliced

In a large bowl, beat cream cheese, sugar, and cornstarch with an electric mixer until smooth. Add eggs one at a time, beating well after each addition. Stir in lemon juice, vanilla extract, and food coloring. Stir in strawberries. Pour filling onto crust. Bake at 350 degrees for 15 minutes.

REDUCE HEAT TO 200 DEGREES and bake for 2 hours, or until center no longer looks wet or shiny. Remove cake from oven and carefully run a knife around inside edge of pan. Turn oven off and return cake to it for an additional 2 hours. Chill overnight.

i ♥ cheesecake

strawberry glaze

5 ounces white chocolate
¼ cup strawberry preserves
whole strawberries, for decoration

In a small heavy saucepan, melt white chocolate over low heat, stirring constantly. Turn heat off and stir in preserves. Spread over cheesecake. Garnish top with strawberries. Chill until serving time.

SWISS WHITE CHOCOLATE
COFFEE CHEESECAKE

mocha cookie crust

18 chocolate creme filled cookies, with fillings intact

2 teaspoons instant coffee, dissolved in 2 teaspoons boiling water

5 tablespoons butter or margarine, melted

Crush cookies to make crumbs. Place crumbs in a mixing bowl then add coffee and butter. Mix thoroughly. Press crumb mixture evenly onto bottom of greased 9-inch cheesecake pan. Set aside.

Have all ingredients at room temperature. Preheat oven to 350 degrees.

coffee white chocolate filling

32 ounces cream cheese

1 cup sugar

3 tablespoons cornstarch

4 large eggs

3 rounded teaspoons instant coffee, dissolved in 1 tablespoon boiling water

½ cup "Swiss White Chocolate" (a naturally and artificially flavored coffee drink mix—this is one of the International Coffees)

½ cup milk, hot, not boiling

2 teaspoons vanilla extract

10 ounces white chocolate, melted

In a large bowl, thoroughly beat cream cheese, sugar, and cornstarch with an electric mixer. Add eggs one at a time, beating well after each addition. Combine dissolved instant coffee and Swiss White Chocolate in milk. Stir this mixture into the batter. Stir in vanilla extract. Stir melted white chocolate into batter, mixing thoroughly. Pour filling onto crust. Bake at 350 degrees for 15 minutes.

REDUCE HEAT TO 200 DEGREES and bake for 2 hours, or until center no longer looks wet or shiny. Remove cake from oven and carefully run a knife around inside edge of pan. Turn oven off and return cake to it for an additional 2 hours. Chill overnight.

coffee white chocolate topping

8 ounces cream cheese
½ cup powdered sugar
4 ounces white chocolate, melted
2 teaspoons instant coffee, dissolved in 2 teaspoons boiling water

In a medium bowl, beat cream cheese and powdered sugar using an electric mixer until smooth. Stir in white chocolate and coffee, mixing thoroughly. Spread topping over cake. Keep chilled.

VANDERMINT CHEESECAKE

This is a cheesecake made from a chocolate mint flavored liqueur.

chocolate mint cookie crust

18 chocolate mint sandwich creme filled cookies, with fillings intact
5 tablespoons butter or margarine, melted

Crush cookies to make crumbs. Place crumbs in a mixing bowl and add butter, mix well. Press crumb mixture evenly onto bottom of greased 9-inch cheesecake pan. Set aside.

Have all ingredients at room temperature. Preheat oven to 350 degrees.

vandermint filling

32 ounces cream cheese
1 cup sugar
3 tablespoons cornstarch
¾ cup Vandermint, or other chocolate mint flavored liqueur
4 large eggs
2 teaspoons vanilla extract

In a large bowl, beat cream cheese, sugar, cornstarch, and Vandermint with an electric mixer until smooth. Add eggs one at a time, beating well after each addition. Stir in vanilla extract. Pour filling onto crust. Bake at 350 degrees for 15 minutes.

REDUCE HEAT TO 200 DEGREES and bake for 2 hours, or until center no longer looks wet or shiny. Remove cake from oven and carefully run a knife around inside edge of pan. Turn oven off and return cake to it for an additional 2 hours. Chill overnight.

i ♥ cheesecake

easy mint topping
1 cup whipping cream
1 tablespoon powdered sugar
1 tablespoon Vandermint
chocolate-covered mints

In a small bowl, beat cream, sugar, and liqueur with an electric mixer until stiff. Spread whipped cream over cake or pipe it around the edge of cake. Garnish with chocolate mints. Refrigerate until serving time.

WHITE CHOCOLATE ORANGE
BIRTHDAY CHEESECAKE

vanilla cookie crust

18 vanilla sandwich creme filled cookies, with fillings intact
5 tablespoons butter or margarine, softened

Crush cookies and make fine crumbs. Please crumbs in a mixing bowl and add butter, mix well. Press crumb mixture evenly onto bottom of greased 9-inch cheesecake pan. Set aside.

Have all ingredients at room temperature. Preheat oven to 350 degrees.

white chocolate orange filling

32 ounces cream cheese
1 cup sugar
3 tablespoons cornstarch
1 teaspoon orange peel, grated
4 large eggs
¾ cup sour cream
8 ounces white chocolate, melted
¼ cup triple sec, or cream
½ teaspoon lemon extract
1 tablespoon orange extract
2 teaspoons vanilla extract

In a large bowl, beat cream cheese, sugar, cornstarch, and orange peel with an electric mixer until smooth. Add eggs one at a time, beating well after each addition. Stir in sour cream and melted chocolate and continue stirring until smooth. Stir in triple sec and lemon, orange, and vanilla extracts. Stir until well blended. Pour filling onto crust. Bake at 350 degrees for 15 minutes.

i ♥ cheesecake

REDUCE HEAT TO 200 DEGREES and bake for 2 hours, or until center is firm and no longer looks wet or shiny. Remove cake from oven and carefully run a knife around inside edge of pan. Turn oven off and return cake to it for an additional 2 hours. Chill overnight.

white chocolate orange topping

8 ounces cream cheese
¼ cup powdered sugar
4 ounces white chocolate, melted
2 teaspoons orange extract
2 drops orange food coloring

In a medium bowl, beat cream cheese and powdered sugar using an electric mixer until well blended and smooth. Stir in white chocolate and continue stirring until evenly mixed. Add orange extract and food coloring, mixing thoroughly. Spread topping over cake. Keep chilled.

notes

candy/cookie

BUTTER RUM CHEESECAKE	58
BUTTERSCOTCH CHEESECAKE	60
CHOCOLATE CANDY CHEESECAKE	62
COOKIES AND CREAM CHEESECAKE	64
PRALINE CHEESECAKE	66
TURTLE CHEESECAKE	68

BUTTER RUM CHEESECAKE

vanilla cookie crust

18 vanilla sandwich creme filled cookies, with fillings intact
5 tablespoons butter or margarine, melted

Crush cookies to make crumbs. Place crumbs in a mixing bowl and add butter, mix well. Press crumb mixture evenly onto bottom of greased 9-inch cheesecake pan. Set aside.

Have all ingredients at room temperature. Preheat oven to 350 degrees.

To get the most rum flavor, be sure to use dark rum in the filling.

butter rum filling

24 ounces cream cheese
⅔ cup dark brown sugar
¼ cup dark corn syrup
3 tablespoons cornstarch
¼ cup dark rum
4 large eggs
1 egg yolk
2 teaspoons vanilla extract
2 teaspoons butter flavoring

In a large bowl, beat cream cheese, brown sugar, corn syrup, cornstarch, and rum with an electric mixer until smooth. Add eggs and yolk one at a time, beating well after each addition. Stir in vanilla extract and butter flavoring. Pour filling onto crust. Bake at 350 degrees for 15 minutes.

REDUCE HEAT TO 200 DEGREES and bake for 2 hours, or until center no longer looks wet or shiny. Remove cake from oven and carefully run a knife around inside edge of pan. Turn oven off and return cake to it for an additional 2 hours. Chill overnight.

i ♥ cheesecake

whipped cream topping

1 cup whipping cream
2 tablespoons powdered sugar
1 teaspoon vanilla extract

In a bowl, beat cream, sugar, and vanilla extract until thickened. Spread whipped cream on cake, creating a design by drawing swirls with bottom of a spoon. Keep chilled.

BUTTERSCOTCH CHEESECAKE

This is a cheesecake from my childhood memories.

vanilla cookie crust

18 vanilla sandwich creme filled cookies, with fillings intact
5 tablespoons of butter or margarine, melted

Crush cookies to make crumbs. Place crumbs in a mixing bowl and add butter, mix thoroughly. Press crumb mixture evenly onto bottom of greased 9-inch cheesecake pan. Set aside.

Have all ingredients at room temperature. Preheat oven to 350 degrees.

butterscotch liqueur filling

24 ounces cream cheese
¾ cup dark brown sugar
3 tablespoons cornstarch
3 large eggs
1 egg yolk
2 teaspoons vanilla extract
2 teaspoons butter flavoring
2 teaspoons butterscotch flavoring
½ cup butterscotch schnapps

In a large bowl, beat cream cheese, brown sugar, and cornstarch with an electric mixer until smooth. Add eggs and yolk one at a time, beating well after each addition. Stir in vanilla extract, butter and butterscotch flavorings, and butterscotch schnapps. Pour filling onto crust. Bake at 350 degrees for 15 minutes.

REDUCE HEAT TO 200 DEGREES and bake for 2 hours, or until center no longer looks wet or shiny. Remove cake from oven and carefully run a knife around inside edge of pan. Turn oven off and return cake to it for an additional 2 hours. Chill overnight.

butterscotch whipped cream topping

1 cup whipping cream

2 tablespoons dark brown sugar

½ cup coarsely crushed butterscotch candies

3 tablespoons chopped pecans (optional)

In a small bowl, beat cream and brown sugar with an electric mixer until stiff. Pipe whipped cream mixture around edge of cake. Sprinkle candies and pecans on top. Keep chilled.

CHOCOLATE CANDY CHEESECAKE

Candy-coated milk chocolate pieces are the candy of choice in this colorful cheesecake.

chocolate cookie and candy crust

18 chocolate sandwich creme filled cookies, with fillings intact
¼ cup candy-coated milk chocolate pieces, chopped
5 tablespoons butter or margarine, melted

Crush cookies to make crumbs. Place crumbs in a mixing bowl and add chopped candy, add butter, mix well. Press crumb mixture evenly onto bottom of greased 9-inch cheesecake pan. Set aside.

Have all ingredients at room temperature. Preheat oven to 350 degrees.

chocolate caramel filling

32 ounces cream cheese
½ cup dark brown sugar
⅓ cup dark corn syrup
3 tablespoons cornstarch
4 large eggs
⅓ cup whipping cream
2 teaspoons vanilla extract
8 ounces milk chocolate chips, melted
1 cup candy-coated milk chocolate pieces

In a large bowl, beat cream cheese, brown sugar, corn syrup, and cornstarch with an electric mixer until smooth. Add eggs one at a time, beating well after each addition. Stir in cream and vanilla extract. Add melted chocolate chips, mix well. Stir in candy. Pour filling onto crust. Bake at 350 degrees for 15 minutes.

i ♥ cheesecake

REDUCE HEAT TO 200 DEGREES and bake for 2 hours, or until center no longer looks wet or shiny. Remove cake from oven and carefully run a knife around inside edge of pan. Turn oven off and return cake to it for an additional 2 hours. Chill overnight.

creamy chocolate topping

3 tablespoons butter or margarine
2 cups sifted powdered sugar
¼ cup unsweetened cocoa
1 teaspoon vanilla extract
1 teaspoon milk
candy-coated milk chocolate pieces

In a small mixing bowl, beat butter until smooth. Gradually add 1 cup powdered sugar and cocoa, beating well. Slowly beat in vanilla extract and milk. Add remaining powdered sugar and beat until smooth. Add more milk, if necessary, for better spreading consistency. Spread chocolate mixture over cheesecake. Garnish with candy. Chill until serving time.

COOKIES AND CREAM CHEESECAKE

Choose your favorite chocolate sandwich creme cookies to use in this filling.

chocolate cookie crust

18 chocolate sandwich creme filled cookies, with fillings intact
3 tablespoons of butter or margarine, melted

Crush cookies to make crumbs. Place crumbs in a mixing bowl and add butter, mix well. Press crumb mixture evenly onto bottom of greased 9-inch cheesecake pan. Set aside.

Have all ingredients at room temperature. Preheat oven to 350 degrees.

triple chocolate filling

32 ounces cream cheese
3 tablespoons cornstarch
1 cup sugar
4 large eggs
⅓ cup crème de cacao
2 teaspoons vanilla extract
8 ounces semisweet chocolate chips, melted
½ cup whipping cream
4 chocolate sandwich creme cookies, coarsely crumbled

In a large bowl, beat cream cheese, cornstarch, and sugar with an electric mixer until smooth. Add eggs one at a time, beating well after each addition. Stir in crème de cacao and vanilla extract. Stir in melted chocolate, mixing thoroughly. Stir in cream. Stir in crumbled chocolate cookies. Pour filling onto crust. Bake at 350 degrees for 15 minutes.

i ♥ cheesecake

REDUCE HEAT TO 200 DEGREES and bake for 2 hours, or until center no longer looks wet or shiny. Remove cake from oven and carefully run a knife around inside edge of pan. Turn oven off and return cake to it for an additional 2 hours. Chill overnight.

chocolate cookie topping

1 cup whipping cream

1 tablespoon sugar

4 chocolate sandwich creme filled cookies, coarsely crumbled.

Put cream and sugar in a small bowl and beat with an electric mixer until stiff. Spread cream over cake. Sprinkle crumbs on top. Keep chilled.

PRALINE CHEESECAKE

This cheesecake will remind you of the classic Southern candy.

vanilla pecan cookie crust

18 vanilla sandwich creme filled cookies, with fillings intact
5 tablespoons pecans, chopped
3 tablespoons butter or margarine, melted

Crush cookies to make crumbs. Place crumbs in a mixing bowl then add pecans and butter. Mix well. Press crumb mixture evenly onto bottom of greased 9-inch cheesecake pan. Set aside.

Have all ingredients at room temperature. Preheat oven to 350 degrees.

caramel praline filling

32 ounces cream cheese
1 cup dark brown sugar
3 tablespoons cornstarch
½ cup dark corn syrup
4 large eggs
2 teaspoons vanilla extract
2 teaspoons butter flavoring
½ cup praline liqueur
⅔ cup pecans, chopped

In a large bowl, beat cream cheese, sugar, cornstarch, and corn syrup with an electric mixer until smooth. Add eggs one at a time, beating well after each addition. Stir in vanilla extract, butter flavoring, and praline liqueur. Stir in pecans. Pour filling onto crust. Bake at 350 degrees for 15 minutes.

i ♥ cheesecake

REDUCE HEAT TO 200 DEGREES and bake for 2 hours, or until center no longer looks wet or shiny. Remove cake from oven and run a knife around inside edge of pan. Turn oven off and return cake to it for an additional 2 hours. Chill overnight.

easy caramel pecan topping

5 ounces white chocolate
¼ cup sour cream
¼ cup caramel flavored ice cream topping (the type that forms a hardened shell)
3 tablespoons pecans, chopped

Place white chocolate and sour cream in a small heavy saucepan. Stir constantly over low heat until chocolate is melted and mixture is smooth. Turn heat off and stir in caramel flavored ice cream topping, stir until evenly mixed. Spread mixture over cheesecake. Sprinkle pecans over top. Keep chilled.

TURTLE CHEESECAKE

chocolate cookie crust

18 chocolate sandwich creme filled cookies, with fillings intact
3 tablespoons pecans, chopped
5 tablespoons butter or margarine, melted

Yes, this decadent cheesecake tastes just like the "turtle" candy!

Crush cookies to make crumbs. Place crumbs in a mixing bowl and add pecans and butter, mix well. Press crumb mixture evenly onto bottom of greased 9-inch cheesecake pan. Set aside.

Have all ingredients at room temperature. Preheat oven to 350 degrees.

chocolate caramel praline filling

32 ounces cream cheese
1 cup dark brown sugar
3 tablespoons cornstarch
⅓ cup dark corn syrup
4 large eggs
2 teaspoons vanilla extract
1¼ teaspoons butter flavoring
3 tablespoons cocoa
¼ cup dark brown sugar
½ cup praline liqueur
½ cup pecans, chopped

In a large bowl, beat cream cheese, 1 cup brown sugar, cornstarch, and corn syrup with an electric mixer until smooth. Add eggs one at a time, beating well after each addition. Stir in vanilla extract and butter flavoring. Remove ¾ cup of mixture and put in a small bowl. To this mixture, add cocoa and ¼ cup brown sugar. Mix well. Set aside. To original mixture, add praline liqueur and blend well. Stir in pecans. Pour half of original mixture onto crust. Spoon on half of cocoa mixture. Pour remainder of original mixture on top of cocoa mixture. Spoon on remaining cocoa mixture. Without disturbing crust, swirl the handle of a knife through cake, creating a marbling effect. Bake at 350 degrees for 15 minutes.

REDUCE HEAT TO 200 DEGREES and bake for 2 hours, or until center no longer looks wet or shiny. Remove cake from oven and run a knife around inside edge of pan. Turn oven off and return cake to it for an additional 2 hours. Chill overnight.

chocolate pecan topping

5 ounces milk chocolate chips
¼ cup sour cream
pecan halves
caramel ice cream topping (the type that forms a hardened shell)

In a small heavy saucepan, combine chocolate and sour cream over low heat, stirring constantly until chocolate is melted and mixture is smooth. Spread on top of cake. Arrange pecan halves over chocolate. Drizzle caramel over pecans and chocolate. Keep chilled.

notes

caramel

CARAMEL APPLE CHEESECAKE	72
CARAMEL CHOCOLATE CHUNK CHEESECAKE	74
CARAMEL MOCHA CHEESECAKE	76
CARAMEL PECAN CHEESECAKE	78
CHOCOLATE CARAMEL PECAN CHEESECAKE	80
SHOOFLY PIE CHEESECAKE	82

SUGAR

NET WT 5LB

CARAMEL APPLE CHEESECAKE

Autumn's favorite flavors are harvested in this mouth-watering cheesecake.

graham cracker crust

2 cups graham cracker crumbs
5 tablespoons butter or margarine, melted
3 tablespoons sugar
¼ teaspoon cinnamon

Place crumbs in a mixing bowl. Add butter, sugar, and cinnamon, mix well. Press crumb mixture evenly onto bottom of greased 9-inch cheesecake pan. Set aside.

Have all ingredients at room temperature. Preheat oven to 350 degrees.

caramel apple pie filling

20 ounce can of apple pie filling
3 large apples, peeled, cored, and sliced
32 ounces cream cheese
¾ cup dark brown sugar
3 tablespoons cornstarch
4 large eggs
1¼ teaspoons cinnamon
2 teaspoons vanilla extract
½ teaspoon lemon extract
½ teaspoon nutmeg
⅔ cup whipping cream or sour cream

Put apple pie filling in a small bowl. Remove 1 or 2 tablespoons of sauce. Stir in fresh sliced apples. In a large bowl, thoroughly beat cream cheese, sugar, and cornstarch with an electric mixer. Add eggs one at a time, beating well after each addition. Add cinnamon, vanilla and lemon extracts, and nutmeg. Stir in whipped cream or sour cream. Pour half of batter onto crust. Spoon on 1 cup of pie filling. With some of remaining batter, make a rim around inside edge of pan, as if to seal filling in. Pour remaining batter over pie filling. Top with remaining pie filling. Without disturbing crust, swirl the handle of a knife through cake to distribute fruit evenly. Bake at 350 degrees for 15 minutes.

REDUCE HEAT TO 200 DEGREES and bake for 2 hours, or until center no longer looks wet or shiny. Remove cake from oven and carefully run a knife around inside edge of pan. Turn oven off and return cake to it for an additional 2 hours. Chill overnight.

caramel frosting

1 tablespoon butter or margarine
⅓ cup dark brown sugar
1¼ teaspoons cream of tarter
2 tablespoons milk
1 teaspoon vanilla extract
¾ cup powdered sugar

In a small heavy saucepan, melt butter. Stir in brown sugar, cream of tarter, and milk, bring to a boil. Turn heat off and cool to lukewarm, about 110 degrees. Stir in vanilla extract and powdered sugar. Beat with an electric mixer until creamy—add a little extra milk if it is too thick. It will thicken after it is on the cake. Spread warm frosting on cake, creating a design. Keep chilled.

CARAMEL CHOCOLATE CHUNK CHEESECAKE

Preheat oven to 350 degrees.

This outstanding caramel cheesecake is topped with chucks of milk chocolate halfway through baking.

nutty oatmeal crust

¾ cup quick rolled oats

¾ cup walnuts or pecans, chopped

¾ cup light brown sugar

½ teaspoon cinnamon

5 tablespoons butter or margarine, melted

In a medium bowl, stir together rolled oats, chopped nuts, brown sugar, and cinnamon. Add melted butter, stirring until well mixed. Press crumb mixture evenly onto bottom of greased 9-inch cheese-cake pan. Bake 18–20 minutes, or until lightly browned. Set aside to cool.

Have all ingredients at room temperature. Keep oven at 350 degrees.

caramel filling

24 ounces cream cheese

⅓ cup dark brown sugar

2 tablespoons cornstarch

2 ounces dark corn syrup

3 large eggs

1 egg yolk

2 teaspoons vanilla extract

1¼ teaspoons butter flavoring

1 cup milk chocolate chunks, or large milk chocolate chips

i ♥ cheesecake

In a large bowl, beat cream cheese, sugar, cornstarch, and corn syrup with an electric mixer until smooth. Add eggs and yolk one at a time, beating well after each addition. Stir in vanilla extract and butter flavoring. Pour filling onto crust. Bake at 350 degrees for 15 minutes.

REDUCE HEAT TO 200 DEGREES and bake for 2 hours, or until center no longer looks wet or shiny. Remove cake from oven and carefully run a knife around inside edge of pan. Sprinkle top with chocolate chunks. Turn oven off and return cake to it for an additional 2 hours. Chill overnight.

CARAMEL MOCHA CHEESECAKE

This is for caramel, chocolate, and coffee lovers!

chocolate cookie crust

18 chocolate sandwich creme filled cookies, with fillings intact
5 tablespoons butter or margarine, melted

Crush cookies to make crumbs. Place crumbs in a mixing bowl and add butter, mix well. Press crumb mixture evenly onto bottom of greased 9-inch cheesecake pan. Set aside.

Have all ingredients at room temperature. Preheat oven to 350 degrees.

mocha caramel filling

24 ounces cream cheese
½ cup dark brown sugar
3 tablespoons cornstarch
3 large eggs
1 egg yolk
2 teaspoons vanilla extract
2 teaspoons instant coffee, dissolved in 2 teaspoons boiling water
3 tablespoons sugar
4 tablespoons dark corn syrup
2 teaspoons butter flavoring
12 ounces milk chocolate chips, melted

In a large bowl, beat cream cheese, brown sugar, and cornstarch with an electric mixer until smooth. Add eggs and yolk one at a time, beating well after each addition. Stir in vanilla extract, mix well. Remove ¾ cup of mixture and put into a small bowl. To this mixture, add dissolved coffee and 3 tablespoons sugar. Mix well. Set aside.

To original mixture, add corn syrup and butter flavoring. Mix well. Thoroughly stir in melted chocolate. Pour half of original mixture onto crust. Spoon on ½ cup of coffee mixture. Pour remainder of original mixture on top of coffee mixture. Spoon on rest of coffee mixture. Without disturbing crust, swirl the handle of a knife through cake, creating a marbling effect. Bake at 350 degrees for 15 minutes.

REDUCE HEAT TO 200 DEGREES and bake for 2 hours, or until center no longer looks wet or shiny. Remove cake from oven and run a knife around inside edge of pan. Turn oven off and return cake to it for an additional 2 hours. Chill overnight.

mocha nut topping

8 ounces cream cheese, softened
2 tablespoons dark brown sugar
2 teaspoons instant coffee, dissolved in 2 teaspoons boiling water
5 ounces milk chocolate chips, melted
4 tablespoons chopped pecans, almonds, or walnuts (optional)

Beat cream cheese, sugar, and dissolved coffee in a medium bowl until smooth. Thoroughly stir in melted chocolate. Spread topping on cake and sprinkle with nuts. Keep chilled.

CARAMEL PECAN CHEESECAKE

*This is
one of my
favorite cheesecakes!*

Preheat oven to 350 degrees.

homemade cookie crust

¾ cup flour

2 tablespoons sugar

1 egg, lightly beaten

4 tablespoons butter or margarine, softened

½ teaspoon vanilla extract

Combine flour and sugar. Add egg, then butter and vanilla extract. Mix well. With generously greased fingers, press dough evenly onto bottom of greased 9-inch cheesecake pan. Bake 12–15 minutes, until lightly browned. Remove from oven and set aside.

Have all ingredients at room temperature. Keep oven at 350 degrees.

caramel pecan filling

24 ounces cream cheese

¾ cup dark brown sugar

⅓ cup dark corn syrup

3 tablespoons cornstarch

3 large eggs

1 egg yolk

2 teaspoons vanilla extract

2 teaspoons butter flavoring

⅔ cup pecans, coarsely chopped

i ♥ cheesecake

In a large bowl, beat cream cheese, sugar, corn syrup, and cornstarch with an electric mixer until smooth. Add eggs and yolk one at a time, beating well after each addition. Stir in vanilla extract and butter flavoring. Stir in chopped pecans. Pour filling onto crust. Bake at 350 degrees for 15 minutes.

REDUCE HEAT TO 200 DEGREES and bake for 2 hours, or until center no longer looks wet or shiny. Remove cake from oven and carefully run a knife around inside edge of pan. Turn oven off and return cake to it for an additional 2 hours. Chill overnight.

caramel pecan frosting

2 tablespoons butter or margarine
⅓ cup dark brown sugar
1¼ teaspoons cream of tarter
2 tablespoons milk
½ teaspoon vanilla extract
¾ cup powdered sugar
⅓ cup pecans, coarsely chopped

In a small heavy saucepan, melt butter. Stir in brown sugar, cream of tarter, and milk. Bring to a boil. Turn heat off and cool to lukewarm, about 110 degrees. Stir in vanilla extract, powdered sugar, and pecans. Beat with electric mixer until creamy—add a little extra milk if it appears too thick. It will thicken after it is on the cake. Spread warm frosting on cake, creating a design by drawing swirls with bottom of a spoon. Keep chilled.

CHOCOLATE CARAMEL PECAN CHEESECAKE

Makes 12–18 slices

This rich, nutty cheesecake tastes just like a candy bar.

chocolate cookie crust

18 chocolate sandwich creme filled cookies, with fillings intact

5 tablespoons butter or margarine, melted

2 tablespoons pecans, chopped

Crush cookies to make crumbs. Place crumbs in a mixing bowl and add butter, mix thoroughly. Press crumb mixture evenly onto bottom of greased 9-inch cheesecake pan and sprinkle pecans on top. Set aside.

Have all ingredients at room temperature. Preheat oven to 350 degrees.

chocolate caramel pecan filling

32 ounces cream cheese

½ cup dark brown sugar

3 tablespoons cornstarch

⅓ cup dark corn syrup

4 large eggs

½ cup sour cream

2 teaspoons vanilla extract

12 ounces milk chocolate chips, melted

⅓ cup pecans, chopped

In a large bowl, beat cream cheese, sugar, cornstarch, and corn syrup with an electric mixer until smooth. Add eggs one at a time, beating well after each addition. Stir in sour cream and vanilla extract. Stir in melted chocolate. Stir in chopped pecans. Pour filling onto crust. Bake at 350 degrees for 15 minutes.

i ♥ cheesecake

REDUCE HEAT TO 200 DEGREES and bake for 2 hours, or until center no longer looks wet or shiny. Remove cake from oven and carefully run a knife around inside edge of pan. Turn oven off and return cake to it for an additional 2 hours. Chill overnight.

chocolate topping

6 ounces milk chocolate chips
⅓ cup sour cream
2 tablespoons dark brown sugar
3 tablespoons pecans, chopped
pecan halves, for decoration
caramel ice cream topping (the type that forms a hardened shell), for garnish

In a small heavy saucepan, mix chocolate, sour cream, and sugar. Melt over low heat, stirring constantly. Remove from heat and stir in pecans. Spread over cheesecake. Arrange pecan halves on top. Drizzle caramel topping over cheesecake. Keep chilled.

SHOOFLY PIE CHEESECAKE

Preheat oven to 350 degrees. Make a cookie crust either with oatmeal cookies or with homemade cookie dough.

Brown sugar and molasses provide the flavor in this crumb-topped cheesecake.

oatmeal cookie crust

22 crisp oatmeal cookies with a 2-inch diameter
3 tablespoons butter or margarine, melted

Crush oatmeal cookies to make crumbs. Place crumbs in a mixing bowl and add butter, mix well. Press crumb mixture evenly onto bottom of greased 9-inch cheesecake pan. Set aside.

homemade cookie dough

¾ cup flour
3 tablespoons sugar
1 egg, lightly beaten
5 tablespoons butter or margarine, softened
1 teaspoon vanilla extract

Mix flour and sugar. Add egg, butter, and vanilla extract, mix well. With generously greased fingers press dough evenly onto bottom of greased 9-inch cheesecake pan. Bake 12–15 minutes, until lightly browned. Remove from oven and set aside.

Have all ingredients at room temperature. Keep oven at 350 degrees.

molasses filling

32 ounces cream cheese
1 cup dark brown sugar
½ cup unsulphured molasses
3 tablespoons cornstarch

½ teaspoon baking soda
4 large eggs
1 tablespoon vanilla extract
2 teaspoons butter flavoring

crumb topping
⅓ cup dark brown sugar
3 tablespoons butter or margarine, melted
⅓ cup flour
3 tablespoons oatmeal

In a large bowl beat cream cheese, brown sugar, molasses, cornstarch, and baking soda with an electric mixer until smooth. Add eggs one at a time, beating well after each addition. Stir in vanilla extract and butter flavoring. Set aside.

In a medium bowl, mix brown sugar, melted butter, flour, and oatmeal. This will resemble coarse meal. Set aside.

Pour batter from first bowl onto crust. Sprinkle crumb topping everly onto batter. Bake at 350 degrees for 15 minutes.

REDUCE HEAT TO 200 DEGREES and bake for 2 hours, or until center no longer looks wet or shiny. Remove cake from oven and carefully run a knife around inside edge of pan. Turn oven off and return cake to it for an additional 2 hours. Chill overnight.

caramel molasses cream topping
⅔ cup whipping cream
2 tablespoons dark brown sugar
½ teaspoon unsulphured molasses

In a bowl, beat cream, brown sugar, and molasses until thickened. Spread whipped cream on cake. Keep chilled.

notes

chocolate

BLACK AND WHITE CHEESECAKE

chocolate cookie crust

18 chocolate sandwich creme filled cookies, with filling intact
5 tablespoons butter or margarine, softened

Crush cookies to make fine crumbs. Place crumbs in a mixing bowl and add butter, mix well. Press crumb mixture evenly onto bottom of greased 9-inch cheesecake pan. Set aside.

Have all ingredients at room temperature. Preheat oven to 350 degrees.

double chocolate filling

32 ounces cream cheese
¾ cup sugar
3 tablespoons cornstarch
4 large eggs
¾ cup sour cream
2 tablespoons vanilla extract
4 ounces white chocolate, melted
1 tablespoon vanilla extract
6 ounces semisweet chocolate chips, melted
¼ cup sour cream
2 tablespoons sugar

In a large bowl, beat cream cheese, ¾ cup sugar, and cornstarch with an electric mixer until smooth. Add eggs one at a time, beating well after each addition. Stir in ¾ cup sour cream and 2 tablespoons vanilla extract. Melt white chocolate in a medium bowl (follow microwave directions found in "Chocolate and Chocolate Substitutes," p. xii). Stir in 1 tablespoon vanilla extract and continue stirring until smooth. Pour one-third of batter into white chocolate mixture, stirring until evenly mixed.

Set mixture aside. Melt semisweet chocolate in a one-quart bowl, using same directions as above. Stir ¼ cup sour cream and 2 tablespoons sugar into this mixture and continue stirring until smooth. Stir semisweet chocolate mixture into remaining batter in original mixing bowl. Using the beater, mix until well blended. Pour half of semisweet batter onto crust. Using the back of a spoon to spread evenly over crust. Pour white chocolate batter over semisweet layer, creating a second layer. As with previous layer, spread evenly. Pour the rest of the semisweet batter over the previous layer and spread evenly. Bake at 350 degrees for 15 minutes.

REDUCE HEAT TO 200 DEGREES and bake for 2 hours, or until center is firm and no longer looks wet or shiny. Remove cake from oven and carefully run a knife around inside edge of pan. Turn oven off and return cake to it for an additional 2 hours. Chill overnight.

double chocolate frosting

8 ounces cream cheese, room temperature
1 cup powdered sugar
4 ounces white chocolate, melted
2 teaspoons vanilla extract
4 ounces semisweet chocolate chips, melted
2 tablespoons powdered sugar
chocolate or caramel ice cream topping (the type that forms a hardened shell) (optional)

In a medium bowl, beat cream cheese and 1 cup powdered sugar with an electric mixer until smooth. In a one-quart bowl, melt white chocolate. After melting, stir in vanilla extract. Set aside. In a second one-quart bowl, melt semisweet chocolate. After melting, stir in 2 tablespoons powdered sugar. Divide cream cheese and powdered sugar evenly between the two chocolate mixtures, mixing each thoroughly. Spread dark chocolate over top of chilled cake. Spread white chocolate over dark chocolate, creating a design on top. After chilling cake, drizzle chocolate ice cream topping over cake. Keep chilled.

BLACK BOTTOM CHEESECAKE

chocolate cookie crust

18 chocolate sandwich creme filled cookies, with fillings intact
5 tablespoons of butter or margarine, melted

This delectable cheesecake is flavored with semisweet chocolate and a hint of rum.

Crush cookies to make crumbs. Place crumbs in a mixing bowl and add butter, mix well. Press crumb mixture evenly onto bottom of greased 9-inch cheesecake pan. Set aside.

Have all ingredients at room temperature. Preheat oven to 350 degrees.

chocolate rum filling

24 ounces cream cheese
2 tablespoons sour cream
⅔ cup sugar
3 tablespoons cornstarch
3 large eggs
1 egg yolk
¼ cup light rum
2 teaspoons vanilla extract
1¼ teaspoons rum flavoring
8 ounces semisweet chocolate chips, melted
⅔ cup whipping cream

In a large bowl, beat cream cheese, sour cream, sugar, and cornstarch with an electric mixer until smooth. Add eggs and yolk one at a time, beating well after each addition. Stir in rum, vanilla extract, and rum flavoring. Add melted chocolate, blending thoroughly. Stir in cream. Pour chocolate rum mixture onto crust. Bake at 350 degrees for 15 minutes.

i ♥ cheesecake

REDUCE HEAT TO 200 DEGREES and bake for 2 hours, or until center is firm and no longer looks wet or shiny. Remove cake from oven and carefully run a knife around inside edge of pan. Turn oven off and return cake to it for an additional 2 hours. Chill overnight.

chocolate rum whipped cream

½ cup whipping cream
1 envelope whipped topping mix
2 tablespoons powdered sugar
1 tablespoon cocoa
¾ teaspoon rum flavoring
maraschino cherries for decoration

In a bowl, combine cream, whipped topping mix, powdered sugar, cocoa, and rum flavoring until well blended. Beat with an electric mixer until stiff. Spread whipped cream over cake. Decorate top with maraschino cherries. Keep chilled.

BLACK FOREST CHEESECAKE

This is an elegant cheesecake.

chocolate cookie crust

18 chocolate sandwich creme filled cookies, with fillings intact
5 tablespoons butter or margarine, melted

Crush cookies to make crumbs. Place crumbs in a mixing bowl and add butter, mix well. Press crumb mixture evenly onto bottom of greased 9-inch cheesecake pan. Set aside.

Have all ingredients at room temperature. Preheat oven to 350 degrees.

chocolate cherry filling

32 ounces cream cheese
1 cup sugar
3 tablespoons cornstarch
4 large eggs
½ cup Bing cherries, pitted, cut, and drained
¼ cup cherry schnapps
2 teaspoons vanilla extract
2 teaspoons cherry flavoring
10 ounces semisweet chocolate chips, melted

In a large bowl, beat cream cheese, sugar, and cornstarch with an electric mixer until smooth. Add eggs one at a time, beating well after each addition. Stir in cherries and cherry schnapps. Stir in vanilla extract and cherry flavoring. Stir in melted chocolate. Stir until well blended. Pour filling onto crust. Bake at 350 degrees for 15 minutes.

REDUCE HEAT TO 200 DEGREES and bake for 2 hours, or until center is firm and no longer looks wet or shiny. Remove cake from oven and carefully run a knife around inside edge of pan. Turn oven off and return cake to it for an additional 2 hours. Chill overnight.

cherry topping

1 cup cherry preserves
2 teaspoons lemon juice
1 teaspoon cornstarch
chocolate ice cream topping (the type that forms a hardened shell)

In a small heavy saucepan, stir together cherry preserves, lemon juice, and cornstarch. Cook and stir over low heat until thickened and bubbly. Cook and stir 2 minutes more. Pour topping over cheesecake. Drizzle chocolate topping over top of cake, creating a design. Keep chilled.

CHOCOLATE CHEESECAKE

This chocolate cheesecake is enveloped in a chocolate glaze and garnished with fresh raspberries and chocolate leaves, if desired.

chocolate cookie crust

18 chocolate sandwich creme filled cookies, with fillings intact
5 tablespoons butter or margarine, melted

Crush cookies to make crumbs. Place crumbs in a mixing bowl and add butter, mix well. Press crumb mixture evenly onto bottom of greased 9-inch cheesecake pan. Set aside.

Have all ingredients at room temperature. Preheat oven to 350 degrees.

semisweet chocolate filling

24 ounces cream cheese
¾ cup sugar
3 tablespoons cornstarch
4 large eggs
1 egg yolk
6 ounces sour cream
2 teaspoons vanilla extract
12 ounces semisweet chocolate chips, melted

In a large bowl, beat cream cheese, sugar, and cornstarch with an electric mixer until smooth. Add eggs and yolk one at a time, beating well after each addition. Stir in sour cream and vanilla extract. Add melted chocolate and mix thoroughly. Pour chocolate cheese mixture onto crust. Bake at 350 degrees for 15 minutes.

REDUCE HEAT TO 200 DEGREES and bake for 2 hours or until center is firm and no longer looks wet or shiny. Remove cake from oven and carefully run a knife around inside edge of pan. Turn oven off and return cake to it for an additional 2 hours. Chill overnight.

chocolate glaze

12 ounces semisweet chocolate chips
2 tablespoons shortening or butter
½ cup powdered sugar
½ teaspoon vanilla extract
fresh raspberries and/or chocolate leaves

In a small heavy saucepan, melt chocolate and shortening over low heat, stirring constantly. Stir in sugar and vanilla extract. Spread over top of cake. Garnish with fresh raspberries and chocolate leaves, if desired. Chill until serving time.

chocolate leaves

Use nontoxic fresh leaves, such as strawberry, mint, lemon, or ivy leaves. Using a small paintbrush, brush melted chocolate on the underside of clean leaves. Place on a baking sheet lined with waxed paper and chill until chocolate hardens. Just before using, peel leaf away from chocolate.

CHOCOLATE BANANA CHEESECAKE

chocolate cookie crust

18 chocolate sandwich creme filled cookies, with fillings intact
5 tablespoons butter or margarine, melted

Crush cookies to make crumbs. Place crumbs in a mixing bowl and add butter, mix thoroughly. Press crumb mixture evenly onto bottom of greased 9-inch cheesecake pan. Set aside.

Have all ingredients at room temperature. Preheat oven to 350 degrees.

chocolate and banana filling

24 ounces cream cheese
¾ cup sugar
3 tablespoons cornstarch
3 large eggs
1 egg yolk
2 teaspoons vanilla extract
2 tablespoons cocoa
3 tablespoons sugar
⅔ cup pureed bananas (2 small bananas)
1 tablespoon banana flavoring

In a large bowl, beat cream cheese, ¾ cup sugar, and cornstarch with an electric mixer until smooth. Add eggs and yolk one at a time, beating well after each addition. Stir in vanilla extract. Remove ¾ cup of mixture and put in a small bowl. To this mixture, add cocoa and 3 tablespoons sugar. Mix thoroughly. Set aside. To original mixture, add pureed bananas and banana flavoring, mixing thoroughly. Pour half of original mixture onto crust. Spoon on ½ cup of cocoa mixture, spreading this out and making it the second layer. Pour remainder of original mixture on top of cocoa mixture and spread. Spoon on remainder of cocoa mixture. Without disturbing the crust, swirl the handle of a knife through the cake, creating a marbling effect. Bake at 350 degrees for 15 minutes.

REDUCE HEAT TO 200 DEGREES and bake for 2 hours, or until center is firm and no longer looks wet or shiny. Remove cake from oven and run a knife around inside edge of pan. Turn oven off and return cake to it for an additional 2 hours. Chill overnight.

chocolate sour cream topping

6 ounces semisweet chocolate chips, melted
⅓ cup sour cream
3 tablespoons powdered sugar
2 tablespoons chopped pecans

In a small heavy saucepan, combine chocolate and sour cream, melt over low heat, stirring constantly. Stir in powdered sugar. Spread over cheesecake. Sprinkle with pecans. Keep chilled.

CHOCOLATE FANTASY CHEESECAKE

This ultimate cheesecake is a chocolate lover's dream come true. Make it when you really want to impress someone.

chocolate cookie crust

18 chocolate sandwich creme filled cookies, with fillings intact
5 tablespoons butter or margarine, melted

Crush cookies to make crumbs. Place crumbs in a mixing bowl and add butter, mix well. Press crumb mixture evenly onto bottom of greased 9-inch cheesecake pan. Set aside.

Have all ingredients at room temperature. Preheat oven to 350 degrees.

triple chocolate filling

32 ounces cream cheese
1 cup sugar
4 large eggs
¼ cup sour cream
¼ cup crème de cacao
2 teaspoons vanilla extract
10 ounces semisweet chocolate chips, melted
4 ounces German sweet chocolate, grated

In a large bowl, beat cream cheese and sugar with an electric mixer until smooth. Add eggs one at a time, beating well after each addition. Stir in sour cream, crème de cacao, and vanilla extract. Stir in melted chocolate chips. Stir in grated German chocolate. Pour chocolate cheese mixture onto crust. Bake at 350 degrees for 15 minutes.

REDUCE HEAT TO 200 DEGREES and bake for 2 hours, or until center is firm and no longer looks wet or shiny. Remove cake from oven and carefully run a knife around inside edge of pan. Turn oven off and return cake to it for an additional 2 hours. Chill overnight.

i ♥ cheesecake

double chocolate whipped cream

¾ cup whipping cream

3 tablespoons powdered sugar

1 tablespoon cocoa

1 teaspoon vanilla extract

1½ ounces German sweet chocolate, grated

2 tablespoons chopped pecans, almonds, or walnuts

In a bowl, beat cream, powdered sugar, and cocoa until it starts to thicken. Add vanilla extract and beat until stiff. Stir in grated German chocolate. Spread whipped cream over cake and decorate with chopped nuts. Keep chilled.

CHOCOLATE MINT SWIRL CHEESECAKE

This colorful cheesecake has 3 layers marbled together.

chocolate cookie crust

18 chocolate sandwich creme filled cookies, with fillings intact
5 tablespoons butter or margarine, melted

Crush cookies to make crumbs. Place crumbs in a mixing bowl and add butter, mix well. Press crumb mixture evenly onto bottom of greased 9-inch cheesecake pan. Set aside.

Have all ingredients at room temperature. Preheat oven to 350 degrees.

chocolate mint filling

24 ounces cream cheese
¾ cup sugar
3 tablespoons cornstarch
4 large eggs
1 egg yolk
2 tablespoons crème de menthe
2 tablespoons rum
2 teaspoons vanilla extract
2 tablespoons crème de cacao
1 tablespoon cocoa
2 tablespoons sugar

In a large bowl, beat cream cheese, ¾ cup sugar, and cornstarch with an electric mixer until smooth. Add eggs and yolk one at a time, beating well after each addition. Remove 1 cup of mixture and put into a small bowl. To this mixture, add crème de menthe. Mix thoroughly and set aside. Remove another 1 cup of mixture and put into a small bowl. To this mixture, add rum and vanilla extract. Mix

i ♥ cheesecake

thoroughly and set aside. To original mixture, add crème de cacao, cocoa, and 2 tablespoons sugar. Mix well. Pour chocolate mixture onto crust. Spoon on crème de menthe mixture, carefully spreading it out and making it the second layer. Spoon on rum mixture and carefully spread it out. Without disturbing crust, carefully swirl the handle of a knife through batter a couple of times. Bake at 350 degrees for 15 minutes.

REDUCE HEAT TO 200 DEGREES and bake for 2 hours, or until center is firm and no longer looks wet or shiny. Remove cake from oven and run a knife around inside edge of pan. Turn oven off and return cake to it for an additional 2 hours. Chill overnight.

mint whipped cream

1 cup whipping cream
1 envelope whipped topping mix
1 tablespoon crème de menthe
chocolate ice cream topping (the type that forms a hardened shell)

Beat cream, whipped topping mix, and crème de menthe until thickened. Spread whipped cream on cake. Drizzle chocolate topping over. Keep chilled.

CHOCOLATE MOUSSE CHEESECAKE

This cheesecake gets its richness from two flavors of chocolate.

chocolate cookie crust

18 chocolate sandwich creme filled cookies, with fillings intact
5 tablespoons butter or margarine, melted

Crush cookies to make crumbs. Place crumbs in a mixing bowl and add butter, mix thoroughly. Press crumb mixture evenly onto bottom of greased 9-inch cheesecake pan. Set aside.

Have all ingredients at room temperature. Preheat oven to 350 degrees.

sweet chocolate filling

24 ounces cream cheese
¾ cup sugar
4 large eggs
¼ cup sour cream
2 teaspoons vanilla extract
10 ounces milk chocolate chips, melted
3 ounces German sweet chocolate, grated

In a large bowl, beat cream cheese and sugar with an electric mixer until smooth. Add eggs one at a time, beating well after each addition. Stir in sour cream and vanilla extract. Stir in melted chocolate chips and grated German chocolate. Mix thoroughly. Pour chocolate cheese mixture onto crust. Bake at 350 degrees for 15 minutes.

REDUCE HEAT TO 200 DEGREES and bake for 2 hours, or until center is firm and no longer looks wet or shiny. Remove cake from oven and carefully run a knife around inside edge of pan. Turn oven off and return cake to it for an additional 2 hours. Chill overnight.

i ♥ cheesecake

chocolate whipped cream

¾ cup whipping cream

2 envelopes whipped topping mix

1 tablespoon cocoa

1 teaspoon vanilla extract

1½ ounces German sweet chocolate, grated

2 tablespoons chopped pecans, almonds, or walnuts

In a bowl, beat cream, whipped topping mix, cocoa, and vanilla extract until it starts thickening. Stir in grated German chocolate. Spread whipped cream over cake and decorate with chopped nuts. Keep chilled.

CHOCOLATE ORANGE CHEESECAKE

chocolate cookie crust

18 chocolate sandwich creme filled cookies, with fillings intact
5 tablespoons butter or margarine, melted

Crush the cookies to make crumbs. Place crumbs in a mixing bowl and add butter, mix thoroughly. Press crumb mixture evenly onto bottom of greased 9-inch cheesecake pan. Set aside.

Have all ingredients at room temperature. Preheat oven to 350 degrees.

creamy orange filling

24 ounces cream cheese
¾ cup sugar
3 tablespoons cornstarch
3 large eggs
1 egg yolk
½ cup frozen concentrated orange juice, thawed
1 tablespoon orange extract
1 teaspoon vanilla extract
1 teaspoon orange peel, finely shredded

In a large bowl, beat cream cheese, sugar, and cornstarch with and electric mixer until smooth. Add eggs and yolk one at a time, beating well after each addition. Stir in orange juice, orange and vanilla extracts, and orange peel. Bake at 350 degrees for 15 minutes.

REDUCE HEAT TO 200 DEGREES and bake for 2 hours, or until center is firm and no longer looks wet or shiny. Remove cake from oven and run a knife around inside edge of pan. Turn oven off and return cake to it for an additional 2 hours. Chill overnight.

i ♥ cheesecake

chocolate sour cream topping

1 cup semisweet chocolate chips
½ cup sour cream
pecan halves

Place chocolate and sour cream in a small heavy saucepan. Stir constantly over low heat until melted and smooth. Drizzle over cheesecake. Garnish with pecans. Chill until serving time.

CHOCOLATE ORANGE SWIRL CHEESECAKE

chocolate cookie crust

18 chocolate sandwich creme filled cookies, with fillings intact
5 tablespoons butter or margarine, melted

Crush cookies to make crumbs. Place crumbs in a mixing bowl and add butter, mix well. Press crumb mixture evenly onto bottom of greased 9-inch cheesecake pan. Set aside.

Have all ingredients at room temperature. Preheat oven to 350 degrees.

orange, almond, and chocolate filling

24 ounces cream cheese
¾ cup sugar
3 tablespoons cornstarch
3 large eggs
1 egg yolk
2 tablespoons orange schnapps
2 teaspoons orange extract
1 drop of orange food coloring
2 tablespoons Amaretto
1¼ teaspoons almond extract
2 tablespoons crème de cacao
2 tablespoons cocoa
2 tablespoons sugar

In a large bowl, beat cream cheese, ¾ cup sugar, and cornstarch with an electric mixer until smooth. Add eggs and yolk one at a time, beating well after each addition. Remove 1 cup of mixture and put into a small bowl. To this mixture, stir in orange schnapps, orange extract, and orange food coloring.

i ♥ cheesecake

Set aside. Remove another 1 cup of mixture and put into a small bowl. To this mixture, stir in Amaretto and almond extract. Set aside. To original mixture, add crème de cacao, cocoa, and 2 tablespoons sugar. Mix well. Pour chocolate mixture onto crust. Spread evenly. Spoon on orange mixture, carefully spreading it out and making it the second layer. Spoon on Amaretto mixture and spread evenly. Without disturbing crust, swirl the handle of a knife through cake a couple of times. Bake at 350 degrees for 15 minutes.

REDUCE HEAT TO 200 DEGREES and bake for 2 hours, or until center is firm and no longer looks wet or shiny. Remove cake from oven and run a knife around inside edge of pan. Turn oven off and return cake to it for an additional 2 hours. Chill overnight.

chocolate orange sour cream topping

½ cup semisweet chocolate chips
3 tablespoons sour cream
2 tablespoons powdered sugar
1 teaspoon orange extract
whole almonds

In a small heavy saucepan, combine chocolate, sour cream, and powdered sugar. Melt over low heat while stirring constantly. Stir in orange extract. Spread over cake and garnish with almonds. Keep chilled.

CHOCOLATE PEANUT BUTTER CHEESECAKE

There is a good chance you will indulge in this outstanding cheesecake time after time.

chocolate cookie crust

18 chocolate sandwich creme filled cookies, with fillings intact
5 tablespoons butter or margarine, melted
3 tablespoons peanuts, chopped

Crush cookies to make crumbs. Place crumbs in a mixing bowl and add butter, mix thoroughly. Press crumb mixture evenly onto bottom of greased 9-inch cheesecake pan. Sprinkle chopped peanuts over crust. Set aside.

Have all ingredients at room temperature. Preheat oven to 350 degrees.

chocolate peanut butter filling

24 ounces cream cheese
½ cup sour cream
¾ cup dark brown sugar
3 tablespoons cornstarch
4 large eggs
½ cup whipping cream
2 teaspoons vanilla extract
2 tablespoons sugar
2 tablespoons cocoa
1 cup creamy peanut butter
⅔ cup peanuts, chopped

In a large bowl, beat cream cheese, sour cream, brown sugar, and cornstarch with an electric mixer until smooth. Add eggs one at a time, beating well after each addition. Stir in whipping cream and vanilla extract. Remove 1 cup of mixture and put into a small bowl. To this mixture, add sugar and

i ♥ cheesecake

cocoa. Mix well and set aside. To original mixture, add peanut butter. Mix well. Stir in chopped peanuts. Pour half of original mixture onto crust. Spoon on half of cocoa mixture and spread evenly, making it the second layer. Pour remainder of original mixture on top of cocoa mixture and spread evenly. Spoon on rest of cocoa mixture. Without disturbing the crust, swirl the handle of a knife through the cake, creating a marbling effect. Bake at 350 degrees for 15 minutes.

REDUCE HEAT TO 200 DEGREES and bake for 2 hours, or until center is firm and no longer looks wet or shiny. Remove cake from oven and run a knife around inside edge of pan. Turn oven off and return cake to it for an additional 2 hours. Chill overnight.

hot fudge topping

6 ounces semisweet chocolate chips
¼ cup butter or margarine
⅔ cup sugar
⅔ cup evaporated milk
¼ cup creamy peanut butter

In a small heavy saucepan, combine chocolate, butter, and sugar. Cook over low heat while stirring constantly. Gradually stir in milk. Bring to a boil then reduce heat. Simmer uncovered for 8 minutes, stirring constantly. Stir in peanut butter until smooth. Remove from heat. Serve warm with cheesecake. Drizzle topping over individual slices.

CHOCOLATE TOFFEE CHEESECAKE

Makes 12–18 slices

This sophisticated cheesecake has a shortbread cookie crust, a rich mocha filling, and a hot fudge topping.

shortbread cookie crust

1¼ cups pecan shortbread cookie crumbs

⅓ cup pecans, chopped

5 tablespoons butter or margarine, melted

Place cookie crumbs and pecans in a mixing bowl and add butter, mix well. Press crumb mixture evenly onto bottom of greased 9-inch cheesecake pan. Set aside.

Have all ingredients at room temperature. Preheat oven to 350 degrees.

mocha filling

32 ounces cream cheese

3 tablespoons cornstarch

1 cup sour cream

1 tablespoon vanilla extract

4 large eggs

½ cup dark brown sugar

3 teaspoons instant coffee, dissolved in 3 teaspoons boiling water

8 ounces milk chocolate chips, melted

½ cup granulated sugar

8 ounces semisweet chocolate chips, melted

In a large bowl, beat cream cheese, cornstarch, sour cream, and vanilla extract with an electric mixer. Add eggs one at a time, beating well after each addition. Remove half of mixture and put into a large bowl. To this mixture, add dark brown sugar and dissolved coffee. Mix well. Add melted milk chocolate chips and mix thoroughly. Set aside. To other half of mixture, add granulated sugar. Add melted

i ♥ cheesecake

semisweet chocolate chips and mix thoroughly. Pour semisweet chocolate mixture onto crust. Spread evenly to create first layer. Spoon on milk chocolate mixture and spread evenly to make second layer. Bake at 350 degrees for 15 minutes.

REDUCE HEAT TO 200 DEGREES and bake for 2 hours, or until center is firm and no longer looks wet or shiny. Remove cake from oven and run a knife around inside edge of pan. Turn oven off and return cake to it for an additional 2 hours. Chill overnight.

hot fudge topping

6 ounces semisweet chocolate chips
2 tablespoons butter or margarine
⅔ cup sugar
⅔ cup evaporated milk
¼ cup chopped chocolate-covered toffee candy bar

In a small heavy saucepan, melt chocolate and butter over low heat, stirring constantly. Add sugar. Gradually stir in milk. Bring to a boil then reduce heat. Simmer uncovered for 8 minutes, stirring frequently. Remove from heat. Serve warm with cheesecake. Drizzle topping over individual slices. Garnish each slice with chopped toffee bars.

GERMAN CHOCOLATE CHEESECAKE

If you are a fan of German chocolate cake, you will love this cheesecake version.

Preheat oven to 350 degrees.

baked chocolate cookie crust

¾ cup flour

1 tablespoon cocoa

¼ cup sugar

1 egg, lightly beaten

5 tablespoons butter or margarine, softened

1 teaspoon vanilla extract

Mix flour, cocoa, and sugar. Add egg, butter, and vanilla extract. Mix well. With generously greased fingers, press dough evenly onto bottom of greased 9-inch cheesecake pan. Bake 12–15 minutes, until lightly browned. Remove from oven and set aside.

Have all ingredients at room temperature. Keep oven at 350 degrees.

german chocolate filling

32 ounces cream cheese

1 cup sugar

3 tablespoons cornstarch

½ cup sour cream

4 large eggs

2 teaspoons vanilla extract

8 ounces of German sweet chocolate, melted

In a large bowl, beat cream cheese, sugar, cornstarch, and sour cream with an electric mixer until smooth. Add eggs one at a time, beating well after each addition. Add vanilla extract and melted chocolate, mixing well. Pour filling onto crust. Bake at 350 degrees for 15 minutes.

i ♥ cheesecake

REDUCE HEAT TO 200 DEGREES and bake for 2 hours, or until center is firm and no longer looks wet or shiny. Remove cake from oven and carefully run a knife around inside edge of pan. Turn oven off and return cake to it for an additional 2 hours. Chill overnight.

coconut pecan topping

4 tablespoons butter or margarine
⅓ cup sugar
⅓ cup evaporated milk
1 egg yolk, lightly beaten
1 cup coconut, grated (reserve ⅓ cup for decoration)
⅔ cup pecans, chopped
2 teaspoons vanilla extract
whole pecans
chocolate bar to make chocolate curls

In a small heavy saucepan, melt butter. Stir in sugar, evaporated milk, and egg yolk. Cook while stirring over low heat until thickened—around 5 minutes. Stir in coconut, chopped pecans, and vanilla extract. Spread over cake. Decorate with reserved coconut and pecans. Use a vegetable peeler to make chocolate curls. Scrape down the edge of the chocolate bar as if you were scraping a carrot. Arrange the curls on the cake. Keep chilled.

MILK CHOCOLATE CHEESECAKE

This is just like eating a big milk chocolate candy bar, only better.

chocolate cookie crust

18 chocolate creme filled cookies, with fillings intact
5 tablespoons butter or margarine, melted

Crush cookies to make crumbs. Place crumbs in a mixing bowl and add butter, mix well. Press crumb mixture evenly onto bottom of greased 9-inch cheesecake pan. Set aside.

Have all ingredients at room temperature. Preheat oven to 350 degrees.

milk chocolate filling

32 ounces cream cheese
1 cup sugar
3 tablespoons cornstarch
¾ cup sour cream
4 large eggs
2 teaspoons vanilla extract
12 ounces milk chocolate chips, melted

In a large bowl, beat cream cheese, sugar, cornstarch, and sour cream with an electric mixer until smooth. Add eggs one at a time, beating well after each addition. Stir in vanilla extract and melted chocolate, mix well. Pour filling onto crust. Bake at 350 degrees for 15 minutes.

REDUCE HEAT TO 200 DEGREES and bake for 2 hours, or until center is firm and no longer looks wet or shiny. Remove cake from oven and carefully run a knife around inside edge of pan. Turn oven off and return cake to it for an additional 2 hours. Chill overnight.

chocolate glaze

5 ounces milk chocolate chips
¼ cup sour cream
1 tablespoon chopped pecans, almonds, or walnuts

In a small heavy saucepan, combine chocolate and sour cream. Stir constantly while melting chocolate over low heat. Spread warm topping on the cake. Sprinkle nuts over top. Keep chilled.

MOCHA SWIRL CHEESECAKE

This show stopper has three swirled flavors: coffee, Amaretto, and crème de cacao.

mocha cookie crust

18 chocolate sandwich creme filled cookies, with fillings intact
5 tablespoons butter or margarine, melted
2 teaspoons instant coffee, dissolved in 2 teaspoons boiling water
3 tablespoons almonds, chopped

Crush cookies to make crumbs. Place crumbs in a mixing bowl and add butter, coffee, and almonds, mixing well. Press crumb mixture evenly onto bottom of greased 9-inch cheesecake pan. Set aside.

Have all ingredients at room temperature. Preheat oven to 350 degrees.

mocha amaretto filling

32 ounces cream cheese
1 cup sugar
3 tablespoons cornstarch
1 tablespoon vanilla extract
4 large eggs
¼ cup coffee flavored liqueur
1 teaspoon instant coffee, dissolved in 1 teaspoon boiling water
¼ cup Amaretto
¼ cup crème de cacao
2 tablespoons cocoa
3 tablespoons sugar

In a large bowl, beat cream cheese, 1 cup sugar, cornstarch, and vanilla extract with an electric mixer until smooth. Add eggs one at a time, beating well after each addition. Remove 1 cup of mixture and put into a small bowl. To this mixture, add the coffee flavored liqueur and the dissolved coffee. Mix thoroughly and set aside. Remove another 1 cup of mixture and put into a small bowl. To this mixture, add the Amaretto. Mix thoroughly and set aside. To the original mixture, add crème de cacao, cocoa, and 3 tablespoons sugar. Mix well. Pour chocolate mixture onto crust and spread evenly to make the first layer. Spoon on the coffee mixture, carefully spreading it out and making it the second layer. Spoon on the Amaretto mixture and carefully spread it out. Without disturbing the crust, swirl the handle of a knife through the cake a couple of times. Bake at 350 degrees for 15 minutes.

REDUCE HEAT TO 200 DEGREES and bake for 2 hours, or until center is firm and no longer looks wet or shiny. Remove cake from oven and run a knife around inside edge of pan. Turn oven off and return cake to it for an additional 2 hours. Chill overnight.

mocha whipped cream topping

½ cup whipping cream
2 envelopes whipped topping mix
2 teaspoons instant coffee, dissolved in 2 teaspoons boiling water
2 tablespoons almonds, chopped

Beat cream and whipped topping mix until it starts to thicken. Add dissolved coffee and continue beating until stiff. Spread topping over cake and top with almonds. Keep chilled.

WHITE FOREST CHEESECAKE

vanilla cookie crust

18 vanilla sandwich creme filled cookies, with fillings intact
5 tablespoons butter or margarine, softened

Crush cookies and make fine crumbs. Place crumbs in a mixing bowl and add butter, mix well. Press crumb mixture evenly onto bottom of greased 9-inch cheesecake pan. Set aside.

Have all ingredients at room temperature. Preheat oven to 350 degrees.

white chocolate cherry filling

32 ounces cream cheese
1 cup sugar
3 tablespoons cornstarch
4 large eggs
¾ cup sour cream
8 ounces white chocolate chips, melted
¾ cup maraschino cherries, pitted and cut in half
¼ cup maraschino syrup
2 tablespoons cherry flavoring
1 tablespoon vanilla extract
1 teaspoon lemon extract

In a large bowl, beat cream cheese, sugar, and cornstarch until smooth with an electric mixer. Add eggs one at a time, beating well after each addition. Stir in sour cream and melted chocolate, and continue stirring until smooth. Add cherries, maraschino syrup, cherry flavoring, and vanilla and lemon extracts. Stir until well blended. Pour chocolate cherry mixture onto crust. Bake at 350 degrees for 15 minutes.

REDUCE HEAT TO 200 DEGREES and bake for 2 hours, or until center is firm and no longer looks wet or shiny. Remove cake from oven and carefully run a knife around inside edge of pan. Turn oven off and return cake to it for an additional 2 hours. Chill overnight.

white chocolate cherry topping

8 ounces cream cheese, room temperature

¼ cup powdered sugar

4 ounces white chocolate, melted

1½ tablespoons cherry flavoring

2 teaspoons vanilla extract

½ cup maraschino cherries, pitted and cut in half

chocolate ice cream topping (the type that forms a hardened shell) (optional)

In a medium bowl, beat cream cheese and powdered sugar with an electric mixer until well blended and smooth. Stir in white chocolate and continue stirring until evenly mixed. Add the cherry flavoring and vanilla extract, mixing thoroughly. Spread topping over cake then place cherries on top, creating a design. After chilling cake, drizzle chocolate ice cream topping over the cake, creating a design. Keep chilled.

notes

coconut

CHOCOLATE COCONUT ALMOND CHEESECAKE	120
COCONUT ALMOND CHEESECAKE	122
COCONUT CHOCOLATE RUM CHEESECAKE	124
COCONUT PINEAPPLE ALMOND CHEESECAKE	126

CHOCOLATE COCONUT ALMOND CHEESECAKE

This multi-flavored cheesecake tastes just like a popular chocolate-covered coconut almond candy bar.

chocolate cookie crust

18 chocolate sandwich creme filled cookies, with fillings intact
5 tablespoons butter or margarine, melted
3 tablespoons almonds, toasted and coarsely chopped

Crush cookies to make crumbs. Place crumbs in a mixing bowl and add butter, mix well. Press mixture evenly onto bottom of greased 9-inch cheesecake pan and sprinkle almonds on top.

Have all ingredients at room temperature. Preheat oven to 350 degrees.

coconut almond filling

24 ounces cream cheese
¾ cup sugar
3 tablespoons cornstarch
3 large eggs
1 egg yolk
½ cup cream of coconut milk
2 teaspoons vanilla extract
1¼ teaspoons almond extract
⅔ cup coconut, flaked or freshly grated
½ cup almonds, toasted and coarsely chopped

In a large bowl, beat cream cheese, sugar, and cornstarch with an electric mixer until smooth. Add eggs and yolk one at a time, beating well after each addition. Stir in cream of coconut milk and vanilla and almond extracts. Stir in coconut and almonds. Pour filling onto crust. Bake at 350 degrees for 15 minutes.

i ♥ cheesecake

REDUCE HEAT TO 200 DEGREES and bake for 2 hours, or until center is firm and no longer looks wet or shiny. Remove cake from oven and run a knife around inside edge of pan. Turn oven off and return cake to it for an additional 2 hours. Chill overnight.

chocolate sour cream topping

6 ounces chocolate chips (milk chocolate or semisweet), melted
⅓ cup sour cream
2 tablespoons powdered sugar
whole or chopped almonds
⅓ cup grated coconut

In a small heavy saucepan, combine chocolate, sour cream, and powdered sugar. Melt over low heat while stirring constantly. Spread warm mixture over cake. Decorate with almonds and coconut. Keep chilled.

COCONUT ALMOND CHEESECAKE

Preheat oven to 350 degrees.

coconut crust

2 cups coconut, flaked or freshly grated
4 tablespoons butter or margarine, melted
4 teaspoons almonds, toasted and coarsely chopped

Place coconut in a mixing bowl and add butter, and almonds, mix well. Press coconut mixture evenly onto bottom of greased 9-inch cheesecake pan. Bake 12–15 minutes or until golden. Set aside.

Have all ingredients at room temperature. Keep oven at 350 degrees.

coconut almond filling

24 ounces cream cheese
⅔ cup sugar
3 tablespoons cornstarch
3 large eggs
1 egg yolk
½ cup cream of coconut milk
2 teaspoons vanilla extract
2 teaspoons almond extract
⅔ cup coconut, flaked or freshly grated
¼ tablespoons almonds, toasted and coarsely chopped

In a large bowl, beat cream cheese, sugar, and cornstarch with an electric mixer until smooth. Add eggs and yolk one at a time, beating well after each addition. Stir in cream of coconut milk and vanilla and almond extracts. Stir in coconut and almonds. Pour filling onto crust. Without disturbing the

i ♥ cheesecake

crust, swirl the handle of a knife through the cake a couple of times to distribute coconut and almonds evenly. Bake at 350 degrees for 15 minutes.

REDUCE HEAT TO 200 DEGREES and bake for 2 hours, or until center is firm and no longer looks wet or shiny. Remove cake from oven and run a knife around inside edge of pan. Turn oven off and return cake to it for an additional 2 hours. Chill overnight.

coconut almond whipped cream

¾ cup whipping cream
3 tablespoons powdered sugar
3 tablespoons coconut, flaked or freshly grated
3 teaspoons almonds, toasted and coarsely chopped
whole almonds
1 maraschino cherry

In a small bowl, combine cream and powdered sugar. Beat with electric mixer for 2–3 minutes until stiff. Spread cream over cake. Sprinkle coconut and chopped almonds on top. Decorate with whole almonds and cherry. Keep chilled.

COCONUT CHOCOLATE RUM CHEESECAKE

Preheat oven to 350 degrees.

coconut crust

2 cups coconut, flaked or freshly grated
4 tablespoons butter or margarine, melted

Place coconut in a mixing bowl and add butter, mix well. Press coconut mixture evenly onto bottom of greased 9-inch cheesecake pan. Bake 12–15 minutes or until golden.

Have all ingredients at room temperature. Keep oven at 350 degrees.

milk chocolate rum filling

24 ounces cream cheese
¾ cup sugar
¾ cup sour cream
4 large eggs
1¼ teaspoons vanilla extract
2 tablespoons rum
12 ounces milk chocolate chips, melted

In a large bowl, beat cream cheese, sugar, and sour cream with an electric mixer. Add eggs one at a time, beating well after each addition. Stir in the vanilla extract, rum, and melted chocolate chips, mixing thoroughly. Pour chocolate cheese mixture onto crust. Bake at 350 degrees for 15 minutes.

REDUCE HEAT TO 200 DEGREES and bake for 2 hours, or until center is firm and no longer looks wet or shiny. Remove cake from oven and carefully run a knife around inside edge of pan. Turn oven off and return cake to it for an additional 2 hours. After removing cake from oven, prepare topping and apply before chilling overnight.

i ♥ cheesecake

warm coconut topping

¼ cup brown sugar

2 tablespoons butter or margarine, softened

2 tablespoons milk

¾ cup flaked coconut

In a bowl, beat brown sugar and butter until smooth. Stir in milk. Stir in coconut. Spread over cake. Broil about 4 inches from heat for 3–4 minutes or until golden. Chill overnight.

COCONUT PINEAPPLE ALMOND CHEESECAKE

Preheat oven to 350 degrees.

coconut crust

2 cups coconut, flaked or freshly grated
3 tablespoons butter or margarine, melted
4 teaspoons almonds, toasted and coarsely chopped.

Place coconut in a mixing bowl then add butter and almonds. Mix well. Press coconut mixture evenly onto bottom of greased 9-inch cheesecake pan and sprinkle with almonds. Bake 12–15 minutes or until golden. Set aside.

Have all ingredients at room temperature. Keep oven at 350 degrees.

pineapple almond filling

24 ounces cream cheese
¾ cup sugar
3 tablespoons cornstarch
3 large eggs
1 egg yolk
2 tablespoons sour cream
1 teaspoon vanilla extract
1 teaspoon almond extract
2 teaspoons lemon juice
½ cup crushed pineapple (fresh or canned), well drained

In a large bowl, beat cream cheese, sugar, and cornstarch with an electric mixer until smooth. Add eggs and yolk one at a time, beating well after each addition. Stir in sour cream and vanilla and almond extracts. Stir in lemon juice and pineapple. Pour filling onto crust. Bake at 350 degrees for 15 minutes.

REDUCE HEAT TO 200 DEGREES and bake for 2 hours, or until center is firm and no longer looks wet or shiny. Remove cake from oven and run a knife around inside edge of pan. Turn oven off and return cake to it for an additional 2 hours. Chill overnight.

pineapple glaze

1 cup pineapple preserves

1 teaspoon cornstarch

2 teaspoons lemon juice

2 tablespoons coconut, flaked or freshly grated

4 teaspoons almonds, toasted and coarsely chopped

In a small heavy saucepan, heat preserves, cornstarch, and lemon juice. Cook and stir over low heat for about 2 minutes until somewhat thickened. Spread hot topping over cake. Sprinkle coconut and almonds on top. Keep chilled.

notes

custard and spice

CARROT CHEESECAKE   130
PUMPKIN CHEESECAKE   132

CARROT CHEESECAKE

This carrot orange dessert rates right up there with the all time favorite carrot cake.

graham cracker crust

2 cups graham cracker crumbs
5 tablespoons butter or margarine, melted
3 tablespoons sugar
½ teaspoon cinnamon

Place crumbs in a mixing bowl and add butter, sugar, and cinnamon. Mix well. Press crumb mixture evenly onto bottom of greased 9-inch cheesecake pan. Set aside.

Have all ingredients at room temperature. Preheat oven to 350 degrees.

carrot orange filling

32 ounces cream cheese
1 cup sugar
3 tablespoons cornstarch
2 teaspoons cinnamon
4 large eggs
3 ounces frozen concentrated orange juice, thawed
2 medium-sized carrots, grated
2 teaspoons vanilla extract
2 teaspoons orange extract

In a large bowl, beat cream cheese, sugar, cornstarch, and cinnamon with an electric mixer until smooth. Add eggs one at a time, beating well after each addition. Stir in orange juice and grated carrots. Stir in vanilla and orange extracts. Pour filling onto crust. Bake at 350 degrees for 15 minutes.

i ♥ cheesecake

REDUCE HEAT TO 200 DEGREES and bake for 2 hours, or until center is firm and no longer looks wet or shiny. Remove cake from oven and carefully run a knife around inside edge of pan. Turn oven off and return cake to it for an additional 2 hours. Chill overnight.

orange pecan frosting

2 tablespoons milk
2 tablespoons butter or margarine
½ teaspoon cinnamon
½ teaspoon orange extract
½ teaspoon vanilla extract
¼ cup pecans or walnuts, chopped
1¼ cups powdered sugar

In a small heavy saucepan, combine milk and butter. Bring to a boil then remove from heat. Put remaining ingredients in a mixing bowl, add milk and butter mixture, and beat well. Pour over hot cake. Keep chilled.

PUMPKIN CHEESECAKE

Makes 12–18 slices

Preheat oven to 350 degrees. Make a cookie crust with either a homemade cookie crust or a refrigerated slice-and-bake sugar cookie dough.

Break away from traditional pumpkin pie and serve this festive cheesecake during the holiday season.

homemade cookie crust

1 cup flour
¼ cup sugar
1 egg, lightly beaten
¼ cup butter or margarine, softened
½ teaspoon vanilla extract

In a bowl, mix flour and sugar. Add egg, then butter and vanilla extract, mix well. With generously greased fingers, press dough evenly onto bottom of greased 9-inch cheesecake pan. Bake 12–15 minutes, until lightly browned. Remove from oven and set aside.

slice-and-bake cookie crust

Use 8 ounces of a roll of slice-and-bake refrigerated sugar cookie dough. Slice as you would to make cookies. With generously greased fingers, arrange in circles, starting on outside edge of pan and working your way in on bottom of greased 9-inch cheesecake pan. Bake as above.

Have all ingredients at room temperature. Keep oven at 350 degrees.

caramel pumpkin filling

32 ounces cream cheese
½ cup dark brown sugar
½ cup granulated sugar
3 tablespoons cornstarch
⅓ cup cocoa (optional)

4 large eggs
1 egg yolk
1½ teaspoons cinnamon
½ teaspoon nutmeg
½ teaspoon ginger
½ teaspoon cloves
2 teaspoons vanilla extract
½ teaspoon lemon extract
8 ounces pumpkin pie filling

In a large bowl, beat cream cheese, brown and granulated sugar, cornstarch, and cocoa with an electric mixer until smooth. Add eggs and yolk one at a time, beating well after each addition. Stir in cinnamon, nutmeg, ginger, and cloves. Stir in vanilla and lemon extracts. Fold in pumpkin. Pour filling onto crust. Bake at 350 degrees for 15 minutes.

REDUCE HEAT TO 200 DEGREES and bake for 2 hours, or until center is firm and no longer looks wet or shiny. Remove cake from oven and carefully run a knife around inside edge of pan. Turn oven off and return cake to it for an additional 2 hours. Chill overnight.

chocolate nut whipped cream
½ cup whipping cream
2 envelopes whipped topping mix
1 tablespoon cocoa (optional)
1 teaspoon vanilla extract
2 tablespoons pecans, chopped
Garnish with cranberries, walnuts, and orange slices

In a bowl, beat cream, whipped topping mix, cocoa, and vanilla extract until stiff. Spread cream over cake. Decorate with pecans and other garnishes. Keep chilled.

notes

fruit

AMBROSIA CHEESECAKE

This luscious cheesecake is spectacular when topped with fresh fruit and drizzled with white and dark chocolate.

Preheat oven to 350 degrees.

coconut crust

2 cups coconut, flaked or freshly grated
4 tablespoons butter or margarine, melted

Place coconut in a mixing bowl and add butter, mix well. Press coconut mixture evenly onto bottom of greased 9-inch cheesecake pan. Bake 12–15 minutes or until golden.

Have all ingredients at room temperature. Keep oven at 350 degrees.

apricot and coconut-flavored filling

24 ounces cream cheese
¾ cup sugar
3 tablespoons cornstarch
½ cup apricot nectar
2 ounces cream of coconut milk
3 large eggs
1 egg yolk
1½ teaspoons vanilla extract
½ teaspoon lemon extract

In a large bowl, beat cream cheese, sugar, and cornstarch with an electric mixer until smooth. Stir apricot nectar and cream of coconut milk into cream cheese mixture. Add eggs and yolk one at a time, beating well after each addition. Stir in vanilla and lemon extracts, blending thoroughly. Pour batter onto crust. Bake at 350 degrees for 15 minutes.

REDUCE HEAT TO 200 DEGREES and bake for 2 hours, or until center is firm and no longer looks wet or shiny. Remove cake from oven and carefully run a knife around inside edge of pan. Turn oven off and return cake to it for an additional 2 hours. Chill overnight.

fresh fruit and chocolate topping

fresh fruit, chopped walnuts
2 ounces white chocolate chips
1 tablespoon light cream
1 teaspoon cherry flavoring
2 ounces semisweet chocolate chips
1 tablespoons light cream

Arrange fresh fruit and walnuts over cheesecake. Chill until serving time. Just before serving, in a small saucepan melt white chocolate chips. Add light cream and cherry flavoring, stirring constantly over low heat. Slice cheesecake and arrange on serving plates. Drizzle melted white chocolate mixture over cheesecake slices. In same saucepan, melt semisweet chocolate and add light cream and stir constantly. Drizzle over cheesecake slices.

APPLE PIE CHEESECAKE

Preheat oven to 350 degrees.

homemade cookie crust

¾ cup flour
¼ cup sugar
½ teaspoon cinnamon
1 egg, lightly beaten
¼ cup butter or margarine, softened
1 teaspoon vanilla extract

In a medium bowl, combine flour, sugar, and cinnamon. Add egg, butter, and vanilla extract, mix well. With generously greased fingers, press cookie dough evenly onto bottom of greased 9-inch cheesecake pan. Bake 15–20 minutes or until lightly browned.

Have all ingredients at room temperature. Keep oven at 350 degrees.

applesauce cream filling

24 ounces cream cheese
¾ cup sugar
3 tablespoons cornstarch
⅔ cup applesauce, sweetened or unsweetened, smooth or chunky
3 large eggs
1 egg yolk
1 teaspoon vanilla extract
1 teaspoon butter flavoring
1 teaspoon cinnamon
¼ teaspoon nutmeg

i ♥ cheesecake

In a large bowl, beat cream cheese, sugar, cornstarch, and applesauce with an electric mixer until smooth. Add eggs and yolk one at a time, beating well after each addition. Add vanilla extract, butter flavoring, cinnamon, and nutmeg. Stir until well blended. Pour batter onto crust. Bake at 350 degrees for 15 minutes.

REDUCE HEAT TO 200 DEGREES and bake for 2 hours, or until center is firm and no longer looks wet or shiny. Remove cake from oven and run a knife around inside edge of pan. Turn oven off and return cake to it for an additional 2 hours. Chill overnight.

apple glaze

½ cup frozen concentrated apple juice, thawed
1 tablespoon lemon juice
1 tablespoon cornstarch
¼ teaspoon cinnamon
1 medium apple, thinly sliced
2 tablespoons lemon juice

In a small heavy saucepan, stir together apple juice concentrate, 1 tablespoon lemon juice, cornstarch, and cinnamon. Cook and stir over low heat until thickened and bubbly. Cook and stir 2 minutes more. Pour warm topping over cake. Toss together apple slices and lemon juice. Arrange on top of cheesecake. Chill until serving time.

APRICOT CHEESECAKE

Fresh apricots and apricot nectar both contribute to the fruity taste of this cheesecake. Look for fresh apricots from late May to early August.

vanilla cookie crust

18 vanilla sandwich creme filled cookies, with fillings intact
5 tablespoons of butter or margarine, melted

Crush cookies to make crumbs. Place crumbs in a mixing bowl and add butter, mix thoroughly. Press crumb mixture evenly onto bottom of greased 9-inch cheesecake pan. Set aside.

Have all ingredients at room temperature. Preheat oven to 350 degrees.

apricot filling

24 ounces cream cheese
¾ cup sugar
3 tablespoons cornstarch
½ cup apricot nectar
3 large eggs
1 egg yolk
½ cup apricots, peeled, pitted, and chopped
2 teaspoons vanilla extract
½ teaspoon lemon extract
1½ teaspoons orange extract

In a large bowl, beat cream cheese, sugar, cornstarch, and nectar with an electric mixer until smooth. Add eggs and yolk one at a time, beating well after each addition. Stir in apricots. Stir in vanilla, lemon, and orange extracts. Pour batter onto crust. Bake at 350 degrees for 15 minutes.

i ♥ cheesecake

REDUCE HEAT TO 200 DEGREES and bake for 2 hours, or until center is firm and no longer looks wet or shiny. Remove cake from oven and carefully run a knife around inside edge of pan. Turn oven off and return cake to it for an additional 2 hours. Chill overnight.

apricot whipped cream

½ cup whipping cream
1 envelope whipped topping mix
2 tablespoons apricot preserves

Put cream and whipped topping mix in a bowl, beating with an electric mixer until stiff. Fold in apricot preserves. Spread on cake, creating a design with the back of a spoon. Keep chilled.

APRICOT MOUSSE CHEESECAKE

Apricot and almond grace this light tasting cheesecake.

vanilla cookie crust

18 vanilla sandwich creme filled cookies, with fillings intact
5 tablespoons of butter or margarine, melted

Crush cookies to make crumbs. Place crumbs in a mixing bowl and add butter, mix thoroughly. Press crumb mixture evenly onto bottom of greased 9-inch cheesecake pan. Set aside.

Have all ingredients at room temperature. Preheat oven to 350 degrees.

apricot almond filling

24 ounces cream cheese
¾ cup sugar
3 tablespoons cornstarch
3 large eggs
1 egg yolk
½ cup apricot preserves
2 tablespoons frozen orange juice concentrate, thawed
2 teaspoons almond extract
1½ teaspoons vanilla extract
½ teaspoon lemon extract
1¼ teaspoons orange extract

In a large bowl, beat cream cheese, sugar, and cornstarch with an electric mixer until smooth. Add eggs and yolk one at a time, beating well after each addition. Stir in apricot preserves, orange juice, and almond, vanilla, lemon, and orange extracts. Mix thoroughly. Pour batter onto crust. Bake at 350 degrees for 15 minutes.

REDUCE HEAT TO 200 DEGREES and bake for 2 hours, or until center is firm and no longer looks wet or shiny. Remove cake from oven and carefully run a knife around inside edge of pan. Turn oven off and return cake to it for an additional 2 hours. Chill overnight.

apricot and orange marmalade whipped cream

½ cup whipping cream
1 envelope of whipped topping mix
½ teaspoon orange extract
½ teaspoon almond extract
2 tablespoons orange marmalade
3 tablespoons almonds, chopped

Put cream, whipped topping, and orange and almond extracts in a bowl. Beat with an electric mixer until stiff. Fold in orange marmalade. Spread on the cake. Sprinkle almonds on top. Keep chilled.

BANANA CREAM CHEESECAKE

Makes 12–18 slices

vanilla cookie crust

18 vanilla sandwich creme filled cookies, with fillings intact
5 tablespoons butter or margarine, melted

Crush cookies to make crumbs and add butter, mix well. Press cookie mixture evenly onto bottom of greased 9-inch cheesecake pan. Set aside.

Have all ingredients at room temperature. Preheat oven to 350 degrees.

This easy-to-make cheesecake will remind you of a rich banana cream pie.

banana cream filling

32 ounces cream cheese
1 cup sugar
3 tablespoons cornstarch
$2/3$ cup pureed bananas (2 small bananas)
4 large eggs
$1/4$ cup banana schnapps
2 teaspoons vanilla extract
2 teaspoons banana extract

In a large bowl, beat cream cheese, sugar, cornstarch, and bananas with electric mixer until smooth. Add eggs one at a time, beating well after each addition. Add banana schnapps and vanilla and banana extracts. Pour batter onto crust. Bake at 350 degrees for 15 minutes.

REDUCE HEAT TO 200 DEGREES and bake for 2 hours, or until center is firm and no longer looks wet or shiny. Remove cake from oven and run a knife around inside edge of pan. Turn oven off and return cake to it for an additional 2 hours. Chill overnight.

banana whipped cream

½ cup whipping cream
1 envelope of whipped topping mix
2 teaspoons banana extract

Beat cream, whipped topping mix, and banana extract with an electric mixer until thickened. Spread topping over cake. Keep chilled.

BANANA SPLIT CHEESECAKE

chocolate cookie crust

18 chocolate creme filled cookies, with fillings intact
5 tablespoons butter or margarine, melted

Crush cookies to make crumbs. Place crumbs in a mixing bowl and add butter, mix thoroughly. Press crumb mixture evenly onto bottom of greased 9-inch cheesecake pan. Set aside.

Have all ingredients at room temperature. Preheat oven to 350 degrees.

This extraordinary cheesecake is the ideal choice for a festive birthday celebration.

banana cream filling

32 ounces cream cheese
¾ cup sugar
3 tablespoons cornstarch
⅔ cup pureed bananas (2 small bananas)
4 large eggs
¼ cup banana schnapps
1¼ teaspoons vanilla extract
2 teaspoons banana extract

In a large bowl, beat cream cheese, sugar, cornstarch, and bananas with an electric mixer until smooth. Add eggs one at a time, beating well after each addition. Add banana schnapps and vanilla and banana extracts. Blend thoroughly. Pour batter onto crust. Bake at 350 degrees for 15 minutes.

REDUCE HEAT TO 200 DEGREES and bake for 2 hours, or until center is firm and no longer looks wet or shiny. Remove cake from oven and run a knife around inside edge of pan. Turn oven off and return cake to it for an additional 2 hours. Chill overnight.

i ♥ cheesecake

pineapple, strawberry, and chocolate topping

sliced banana
fresh pineapple chunks
fresh strawberries, sliced
chocolate syrup

Place pieces of fresh fruit on top of cake. Warm chocolate syrup and drizzle on top.

or

whipped cream topping

½ cup whipping cream
2 envelopes non-dairy whipped topping mix
½ sliced banana
½ cup sliced strawberries, well drained
¼ cup crushed pineapple, well drained
¼ cup sliced maraschino cherries
3 tablespoons pecans, whole or chopped
chocolate ice cream topping (the type that forms a hardened shell)

Beat cream and whipped topping mix together until thickened. Spread whipped cream over cake. Decorate and create a design with fruit and nuts. Drizzle ice cream topping on top. Keep chilled.

BANANAS FOSTER CHEESECAKE

Makes 12–18 slices

Bananas, rum, and brown sugar make this delightful cheesecake taste like the classic dessert.

vanilla cookie crust

18 vanilla sandwich creme filled cookies, with fillings intact
5 tablespoons butter or margarine, melted

Crush cookies to make crumbs, add butter, mix well. Press cookie mixture evenly onto bottom of greased 9-inch cheesecake pan.

Have all ingredients at room temperature. Preheat oven to 350 degrees.

caramel banana filling

24 ounces cream cheese
¾ cup dark brown sugar
3 tablespoons cornstarch
¾ teaspoon cinnamon
⅔ cup pureed bananas (2 small bananas)
3 large eggs
1 egg yolk
3 tablespoons light rum
2 teaspoons vanilla extract
1 tablespoon banana extract

In a large bowl, beat cream cheese, brown sugar, cornstarch, cinnamon, and pureed bananas with an electric mixer until smooth. Add eggs and yolk one at a time, beating well after each addition. Stir in rum and vanilla and banana extracts, mix well. Pour batter onto crust. Bake at 350 degrees for 15 minutes.

i ♥ cheesecake

REDUCE HEAT TO 200 DEGREES and bake for 2 hours, or until center is firm and no longer looks wet or shiny. Remove cake from oven and run a knife around inside edge of pan. Turn oven off and return cake to it for an additional 2 hours. Chill overnight.

banana whipped cream

½ cup whipping cream

1 envelope whipped topping mix

2 tablespoons dark brown sugar

2 teaspoons banana extract

1 small banana, sliced and dipped in lemon juice

Beat cream, whipped topping mix, brown sugar, and banana extract until thickened. Spread whipped cream over cake, creating a design with back of a spoon. Decorate with sliced banana. Keep chilled.

BING CHERRY CHEESECAKE

Makes 12–18 slices

Chocolate and cherries are a classic combination. Try this easy version when fresh Bing cherries are in season (mid-May to mid-August).

graham cracker crust

2 cups graham cracker crumbs
5 tablespoons butter or margarine, melted
¼ cup sugar

Place crumbs in a mixing bowl then add butter and sugar. Mix well. Press crumb mixture evenly onto bottom of greased 9-inch cheesecake pan. Set aside.

Have all ingredients at room temperature. Preheat oven to 350 degrees.

cherry filling

32 ounces cream cheese
1 cup sugar
3 tablespoons cornstarch
4 large eggs
¼ cup cherry liqueur, such as Kirsch
2 teaspoons cherry flavoring
2 teaspoons vanilla extract
2 drops red food coloring

In a large bowl, beat cream cheese, sugar, and cornstarch with an electric mixer until smooth. Add eggs one at a time, beating well after each addition. Stir in cherry liqueur, cherry flavoring, vanilla extract, and food coloring. Mix well. Pour batter onto crust. Bake at 350 degrees for 15 minutes.

REDUCE HEAT TO 200 DEGREES and bake for 2 hours, or until center is firm and no longer looks wet or shiny. Remove cake from oven and run a knife around inside edge of pan. Turn oven off and return cake to it for an additional 2 hours. Chill overnight.

i ♥ cheesecake

cherry topping

14 ounces Bing cherries (fresh or canned), pitted and drained

1 tablespoon cornstarch

1 tablespoon lemon juice

3 tablespoons sugar

2 teaspoons cherry flavoring

1 drop red food coloring

In a small heavy saucepan, combine cherries, cornstarch, and lemon juice. Stir in sugar, cherry flavoring, and red food coloring. Blend well. Cook and stir over low heat until thickened—about 5 minutes. Spread topping over cake while topping is still warm. Keep chilled.

BLACKBERRY CHEESECAKE

Blackberries and sweet blackberry wine give this cheesecake its berry boost.

vanilla cookie crust

18 vanilla sandwich creme filled cookies, with fillings intact
5 tablespoons butter or margarine, melted
2 tablespoons almonds, toasted and coarsely chopped (optional)

Crush cookies to make crumbs. Place crumbs in a mixing bowl and add butter, mix well. Press crumb mixture evenly onto bottom of greased 9-inch cheesecake pan. Sprinkle with almonds. Set aside.

Have all ingredients at room temperature. Preheat oven to 350 degrees.

blackberry almond filling

24 ounces cream cheese
¾ cup sugar
3 tablespoons cornstarch
3 large eggs
1 egg yolk
2 teaspoons almond extract
2 teaspoons vanilla extract
½ teaspoon lemon extract
½ teaspoon cinnamon
½ cup fresh or frozen blackberries, thawed and well drained
4 tablespoons almonds, toasted and coarsely chopped (optional)
1½ ounces sweet blackberry wine

In a large bowl, beat cream cheese, sugar, and cornstarch with an electric mixer until smooth. Add eggs and yolk one at a time, beating well after each addition. Stir in almond, vanilla, and lemon extracts

152

and cinnamon. Stir in blackberries, almonds, and blackberry wine. Mix well. Pour batter onto crust. Bake at 350 degrees for 15 minutes.

REDUCE HEAT TO 200 DEGREES and bake for 2 hours, or until center is firm and no longer looks wet or shiny. Remove cake from oven and carefully run a knife around inside edge of pan. Turn oven off and return cake to it for an additional 2 hours. Chill overnight.

warm blackberry topping

½ cup blackberry preserves, jelly or jam
3 tablespoons almonds, toasted and coarsely chopped (optional)

Immediately before serving, heat preserves. Stir constantly. Spread topping on cake and sprinkle blackberries and almonds on top.

BLUEBERRY CHEESECAKE

Make this a tradition when fresh blueberries are in season (June–August).

graham cracker crust

2 cups graham cracker crumbs
5 tablespoons butter or margarine, melted
3 tablespoons sugar

Place crumbs in a mixing bowl and add butter and sugar. Mix thoroughly. Press crumb mixture evenly onto bottom of greased 9-inch cheesecake pan. Set aside.

Have all ingredients at room temperature. Preheat oven to 350 degrees.

blueberry filling

24 ounces cream cheese
¾ cup sugar
3 tablespoons cornstarch
3 large eggs
1 egg yolk
1¼ teaspoons lemon extract
1¼ teaspoons vanilla extract
¾ cup fresh, frozen or canned blueberries, well drained

In a large bowl, beat cream cheese, sugar, and cornstarch with an electric mixer until smooth. Add eggs and yolk one at a time, beating well after each addition. Stir in lemon and vanilla extracts and blueberries. Pour batter onto crust. Bake at 350 degrees for 15 minutes.

REDUCE HEAT TO 200 DEGREES and bake for 2 hours, or until center is firm and no longer looks wet or shiny. Remove from oven and carefully run a knife around inside edge of pan. Turn oven off and return cake to it for an additional 2 hours. Chill overnight.

i ♥ cheesecake

blueberry topping

¾ cup blueberry preserves
2 teaspoons cornstarch
2 teaspoons lemon juice

In a small heavy saucepan, combine preserves, cornstarch, and lemon juice. Cook and stir over low heat until thickened and bubbly. Cool slightly and spread over cake. Keep chilled.

CHERRY ALMOND CHEESECAKE

Makes 12–18 slices

Cherries are available from mid-May to mid-August. Be sure to toast the almonds for a nuttier flavor and a crunchier texture.

graham cracker crust

2 cups graham cracker crumbs
5 tablespoons butter or margarine, melted
3 tablespoons almonds, chopped
3 tablespoons sugar

Place crumbs in a mixing bowl and add butter, almonds, and sugar. Mix well. Press crumb mixture evenly onto bottom of greased 9-inch cheesecake pan. Set aside.

Have all ingredients at room temperature. Preheat oven to 350 degrees.

cherry filling

18 ounces fresh Bing cherries, pitted
⅔ cup sugar
1 tablespoon cornstarch
32 ounces cream cheese
1 cup sugar
3 tablespoons cornstarch
4 large eggs
1 tablespoon lemon juice
2 teaspoons almond extract
1 teaspoon vanilla extract
⅓ cup chopped almonds, toasted

In a small heavy saucepan, stir together cherries and ⅔ cup sugar. Let stand 30 minutes. Stir in 1 tablespoon cornstarch. Cook and stir until thickened. Set aside.

In a large bowl, beat cream cheese, 1 cup sugar, and 3 tablespoons cornstarch with an electric mixer until smooth. Add eggs one at a time, beating well after each addition. Stir in lemon juice and almond and vanilla extracts. Stir in almonds. Pour batter onto crust. Bake at 350 degrees for 15 minutes.

REDUCE HEAT TO 200 DEGREES and bake for 2 hours, or until center is firm and no longer looks wet or shiny. Remove cake from oven and carefully run a knife around inside edge of pan. Turn oven off and return cake to it for an additional 2 hours. Chill overnight.

easy cherry topping

1 cup cherry preserves
2 teaspoons lemon juice
1¼ teaspoons almond extract
⅓ cup almonds, toasted and chopped

In a small heavy saucepan, heat preserves and lemon juice over low heat, stirring constantly. Cook and stir until bubbly and thickened. Remove from heat and stir in almond extract. Immediately before serving, put topping on cake. Sprinkle with almonds.

CHOCOLATE CHERRY ALMOND CHEESECAKE

chocolate cookie crust

18 chocolate sandwich creme filled cookies, with fillings intact

5 tablespoons butter or margarine, melted

3 tablespoons almonds, chopped

This cheesecake has a chocolate crust and a swirled chocolate and cherry filling.

Crush cookies to make crumbs. Place crumbs in a mixing bowl and add butter, mix thoroughly. Press crumb mixture evenly onto bottom of greased 9-inch cheesecake pan. Sprinkle with chopped almonds. Set aside.

Have all ingredients at room temperature. Preheat oven to 350 degrees.

chocolate cherry filling

32 ounces cream cheese

1 cup sugar

3 tablespoons cornstarch

4 large eggs

2 teaspoons vanilla extract

2 tablespoons cocoa

3 tablespoons sugar

¼ cup cherry schnapps

1 tablespoon cherry flavoring

½ teaspoon lemon extract

1½ teaspoons almond extract

⅔ cup Bing cherries, chopped, pitted, and well drained

In a large bowl, beat cream cheese, 1 cup sugar, and cornstarch with an electric mixer until smooth. Add eggs one at a time, beating well after each addition. Stir in vanilla extract. Remove 1 cup of mixture and put in a small bowl. To this mixture, add cocoa and 3 tablespoons sugar, mix well. Set aside. To original mixture, add cherry schnapps, mixing thoroughly. Stir in cherry flavoring and lemon and almond extracts. Fold in chopped Bing cherries. Pour half of original mixture onto crust. Spoon on ½ cup of cocoa mixture; spread this out evenly, making it the second layer. Pour remaining original mixture on top of cocoa mixture, spreading this out also. Spoon on rest of cocoa mixture. Without disturbing crust, swirl the handle of a knife through cake, creating a marbling effect. Bake at 350 degrees for 15 minutes.

REDUCE HEAT TO 200 DEGREES and bake for 2 hours, or until center is firm and no longer looks wet or shiny. Remove cake from oven and run a knife around inside edge of pan. Turn oven off and return cake to it for an additional 2 hours. Chill overnight.

chocolate cherry almond topping

6 ounces milk chocolate chips
⅓ cup sour cream
2 tablespoons powdered sugar
¼ cup Bing cherries, chopped, pitted, and well drained
3 tablespoons almonds, chopped

In a small heavy saucepan, combine chocolate chips, sour cream, and powdered sugar, stirring constantly over low heat until melted and smooth. Stir in chopped Bing cherries and almonds. Spread over cake while chocolate is hot. Keep chilled.

CRANBERRY ORANGE CHEESECAKE

Makes 12–18 slices

This beautiful cheesecake is great for the holidays but can be made all year.

vanilla wafer crust

2 cups vanilla wafers

¼ cup butter or margarine, melted

3 tablespoons walnuts, chopped

Crush wafers to make crumbs. Place crumbs in a mixing bowl and add butter, mix well. Press crumb mixture evenly onto bottom of greased 9-inch cheesecake pan. Sprinkle with chopped walnuts. Set aside.

Have all ingredients at room temperature. Preheat oven to 350 degrees.

cranberry filling

24 ounces cream cheese

¾ cup sugar

3 tablespoons cornstarch

3 large eggs

1 egg yolk

1 teaspoon vanilla extract

1¼ teaspoons orange extract

¼ cup frozen concentrated cranberry juice cocktail, thawed

1 cup fresh cranberries, chopped

⅓ cup walnuts, chopped

In a large bowl, beat cream cheese, sugar, and cornstarch with an electric mixer until smooth. Add eggs and yolk one at a time, beating well after each addition. Stir in vanilla and orange extracts. Stir in cranberry juice. Put cranberries and walnuts in a blender or food processor and chop fine. Add mixture to cream cheese, mixing well. Pour batter onto crust. Bake at 350 degrees for 15 minutes.

i ♥ cheesecake

REDUCE HEAT TO 200 DEGREES and bake for 2 hours, or until center is firm and no longer looks wet or shiny. Remove cake from oven and carefully run a knife around inside edge of pan. Turn oven off and return cake to it for an additional 2 hours. Chill overnight.

cranberry orange glaze

1 cup orange marmalade

5 tablespoons fresh cranberries, chopped

2 teaspoons cornstarch

3 tablespoons walnuts, chopped

In a small heavy saucepan, heat marmalade, cranberries, and cornstarch. Cook over low heat, stirring constantly until thickened—about 2 minutes. Spread warm topping on cake. Sprinkle walnuts over top. Keep chilled.

CREAMY LEMON CHEESECAKE

graham cracker crust

2 cups graham cracker crumbs

5 tablespoons butter or margarine, melted

3 tablespoons sugar

Place crumbs in a mixing bowl and add butter and sugar, mix well. Press crumb mixture evenly onto bottom of greased 9-inch cheesecake pan. Set aside.

Have all ingredients at room temperature. Preheat oven to 350 degrees.

creamy lemon filling

24 ounces cream cheese

¾ cup sugar

3 tablespoons cornstarch

3 large eggs

1 egg yolk

2 teaspoons vanilla extract

2 teaspoons lemon extract

½ cup sour cream

4 ounces frozen concentrated lemonade, thawed

1 teaspoon lemon peel, finely grated

In large bowl, beat cream cheese, sugar, and cornstarch with an electric mixer until smooth. Add eggs and yolk one at a time, beating well after each addition. Add vanilla and lemon extracts, mix well. Stir in sour cream, lemonade, and lemon peel. Pour batter onto crust. Bake at 350 degrees for 15 minutes.

REDUCE HEAT TO 200 DEGREES and bake for 2 hours, or until center is firm and no longer looks wet or shiny. Remove cake from oven and run a knife around inside edge of pan. Turn oven off and return cake to it for an additional 2 hours. Chill overnight.

lemon topping

8 ounces white chocolate chips
4 ounces sour cream
1¼ teaspoons lemon extract
1 drop of yellow food coloring

In a small heavy saucepan, combine white chocolate, sour cream, lemon extract, and food coloring. Stir constantly over low heat until melted and smooth. Spread topping over cake. Keep chilled.

CREAMY ORANGE CHEESECAKE

This citrus cheesecake tastes like a cross between orange sherbet and an Orange Julius.

vanilla cookie crust

18 vanilla sandwich creme filled cookies, with fillings intact
5 tablespoons butter or margarine, melted

Crush cookies to make crumbs. Place crumbs in a mixing bowl and add butter, mix well. Press crumb mixture evenly onto bottom of greased 9-inch cheesecake pan. Set aside.

Have all ingredients at room temperature. Preheat oven to 350 degrees.

creamy orange filling

32 ounces cream cheese
1 cup sugar
4 tablespoons cornstarch
4 large eggs
6 ounces frozen orange juice concentrate, thawed
2 teaspoons orange extract
1¼ teaspoons vanilla extract
1 teaspoon orange peel, finely grated
2 drops orange food coloring (optional)

In a large bowl, beat cream cheese, sugar, and cornstarch with an electric mixer until smooth. Add eggs one at a time, beating well after each addition. Add orange juice, orange and vanilla extracts, orange peel, and food coloring. Mix thoroughly. Pour batter onto crust. Bake at 350 degrees for 15 minutes.

i ♥ cheesecake

REDUCE HEAT TO 200 DEGREES and bake for 2 hours, or until center is firm and no longer looks wet or shiny. Remove cake from oven and carefully run a knife around inside edge of pan. Turn oven off and return cake to it for an additional 2 hours. Chill overnight.

creamy orange topping

8 ounces cream cheese

½ cup powdered sugar

4 ounces white chocolate, melted

1 teaspoon orange extract

1 drop orange food coloring (optional)

In a medium bowl, beat cream cheese and powdered sugar with an electric mixer until smooth. Stir in chocolate, orange extract, and food coloring. Decorate top of cake with topping. Keep chilled.

FRESH PINEAPPLE CHEESECAKE

Makes 12–18 slices

vanilla cookie crust

18 vanilla sandwich creme filled cookies, with fillings intact
5 tablespoons butter or margarine, melted

Look for cored and peeled pineapple in your grocer's produce section.

Crush cookies and make crumbs. Place crumbs in a mixing bowl, add butter, mix well. Press cookie mixture evenly onto bottom of greased 9-inch cheesecake pan. Set aside.

Have all ingredients at room temperature. Preheat oven to 350 degrees.

pineapple filling

32 ounces cream cheese
1 cup sugar
3 tablespoons cornstarch
4 large eggs
1 teaspoon vanilla extract
½ teaspoon lemon extract
½ cup frozen concentrated pineapple juice, thawed
1 cup pineapple, fresh, cored, peeled and finely chopped

In a large bowl, beat cream cheese, sugar, and cornstarch with an electric mixer until smooth. Add eggs one at a time, beating well after each addition. Stir in vanilla and lemon extracts. Stir in pineapple juice and pineapple. Pour batter onto crust. Without disturbing crust, swirl the handle of a knife through batter, creating an even distribution of pineapple. Bake at 350 degrees for 15 minutes.

REDUCE HEAT TO 200 DEGREES and bake for 2 hours, or until center is firm and no longer looks wet or shiny. Remove cake from oven and run a knife around inside edge of pan. Turn oven off and return cake to it for an additional 2 hours. Chill overnight.

i ♥ cheesecake

6 ounces white chocolate
1 cup pineapple preserves

In a small heavy saucepan, stir together chocolate and pineapple preserves over low heat. Continue stirring until hot and chocolate has melted. Spread over cake while topping is still hot. Chill until serving time.

IMPERIAL BING CHERRY CHEESECAKE

graham cracker crust

2 cups graham cracker crumbs

5 tablespoons butter or margarine, melted

3 tablespoons sugar

Place crumbs in a mixing bowl and add butter and sugar, mix well. Press crumb mixture evenly onto bottom of greased 9-inch cheesecake pan. Set aside.

Have all ingredients at room temperature. Preheat oven to 350 degrees.

bing cherry filling

32 ounces cream cheese

1 cup sugar

3 tablespoons cornstarch

4 large eggs

¼ cup cherry liqueur, such as Kirsch

2 teaspoons cherry flavoring

2 teaspoons vanilla extract

¼ teaspoon lemon extract

9 ounces Bing cherries (fresh or canned), pitted, chopped, and well drained

In a large bowl, beat cream cheese, sugar, and cornstarch with an electric mixer until smooth. Add eggs one at a time, beating well after each addition. Stir in cherry liqueur, cherry flavoring, and vanilla and lemon extracts. Pour half of batter onto crust. Spoon on 7 ounces of drained cherries. With part of remaining batter, make a rim around inside edge of pan as if to seal the cherries in. Pour remaining batter over cherries. Spoon on remainder of cherries, spreading them out. Bake at 350 degrees for 15 minutes.

i ♥ cheesecake

REDUCE HEAT TO 200 DEGREES and bake for 2 hours, or until center is firm and no longer looks wet or shiny. Remove cake from oven and run a knife around inside edge of pan. Turn oven off and return cake to it for an additional 2 hours. Chill overnight.

cherry topping

10 ounces cherry preserves
2 teaspoons cornstarch
½ teaspoon lemon juice
½ teaspoon almond extract
1¼ teaspoons cherry flavoring
3 tablespoons almonds, chopped
2 tablespoons maraschino cherries, chopped

In a small heavy saucepan, combine preserves, cornstarch, and lemon juice. Cook over low heat, stirring constantly until thickened. Stir in almond extract and cherry flavoring. Spread warm topping on cake. Sprinkle chopped almonds and maraschino cherries on top. Keep chilled.

KEY LIME, KEY WEST TRADITION CHEESECAKE

A Key West, Florida, Tradition!

vanilla cookie crust

18 vanilla sandwich creme filled cookies, with fillings intact
5 tablespoons butter or margarine, melted

Crush cookies to make crumbs. Place crumbs in a mixing bowl and add butter, mix thoroughly. Press crumb mixture evenly onto bottom of greased 9-inch cheesecake pan. Set aside.

Have all ingredients at room temperature. Preheat oven to 350 degrees.

key lime filling

32 ounces cream cheese
14 ounces sweetened condensed milk
1 cup sugar
3 tablespoons cornstarch
4 large eggs
¾ cup key lime juice
2 teaspoons vanilla extract
12 ounces white chocolate, melted

In a large bowl, beat cream cheese, sweetened condensed milk, sugar, and cornstarch with an electric mixer until smooth. Add eggs one at a time, beating well after each addition. Stir in key lime juice and vanilla extract. Stir in melted chocolate. Pour batter onto crust, spreading evenly. Bake at 350 degrees for 15 minutes.

i ♥ cheesecake

REDUCE HEAT TO 200 DEGREES and bake for 2 hours, or until center is firm and no longer looks wet or shiny. Remove cake from oven and carefully run a knife around inside edge of pan. Turn oven off and return cake to it for an additional 2 hours. Chill overnight.

white chocolate lime topping

4 ounces cream cheese
½ cup powdered sugar
5 ounces white chocolate, melted
1 teaspoon key lime juice

In a medium bowl, beat cream cheese and powdered sugar with an electric mixer until smooth. Stir melted white chocolate into cream cheese mixture. Add lime juice. Mix thoroughly and decorate cake. Keep chilled.

LEMON DROP CHEESECAKE

Makes 12–18 slices

Serve this light tasting cheesecake on a sultry day.

graham cracker crust

2 cups graham cracker crumbs
5 tablespoons butter or margarine, melted
3 tablespoons sugar

Place crumbs in a mixing bowl and add butter and sugar, mix well. Press crumb mixture evenly onto bottom of greased 9-inch cheesecake pan. Set aside.

Have all ingredients at room temperature. Preheat oven to 350 degrees.

lemon filling

32 ounces cream cheese
1 cup sugar
3 tablespoons cornstarch
6 ounces frozen concentrated lemonade, thawed
4 large eggs
2 teaspoons vanilla extract
2 teaspoons lemon extract
2 drops of yellow food coloring

In a large bowl, beat cream cheese, sugar, and cornstarch with an electric mixer until smooth. Stir in lemonade. Add eggs one at a time, beating well after each addition. Add vanilla and lemon extracts and food coloring. Mix well. Pour batter onto crust. Bake at 350 degrees for 15 minutes.

REDUCE HEAT TO 200 DEGREES and bake for 2 hours, or until center is firm and no longer looks wet or shiny. Remove cake from oven and run a knife around inside edge of pan. Turn oven off and return cake to it for an additional 2 hours. Chill overnight.

i ♥ cheesecake

lemon whipped cream

1 cup whipping cream
1 envelope whipped topping mix
1 teaspoon lemon extract
1 drop of yellow food coloring
1 teaspoon lemon peel, finely grated

In a small bowl, combine whipping cream, whipped topping mix, and lemon extract. Stir in food coloring, mix well. Beat with an electric mixer until stiff. Spread over cake. Sprinkle grated lemon peel over cream topping. Keep chilled.

LIMON CHEESECAKE

This is a blend of lime and lemon.

graham cracker crust

2 cups graham cracker crumbs

5 tablespoons butter or margarine, melted

3 tablespoons sugar

Place crumbs in a mixing bowl and add butter and sugar, mix well. Press crumb mixture evenly onto bottom of greased 9-inch cheesecake pan. Set aside.

Have all ingredients at room temperature. Preheat oven to 350 degrees.

lemon lime filling

32 ounces cream cheese

1 cup sugar

3 tablespoons cornstarch

4 large eggs

2 teaspoons vanilla extract

1¼ teaspoons lemon extract

½ cup frozen concentrated limeade, thawed

½ cup frozen concentrated lemonade, thawed

In a large bowl, beat cream cheese, sugar, and cornstarch with an electric mixer until smooth. Add eggs one at a time, beating well after each addition. Stir in vanilla and lemon extracts. Stir in limeade and lemonade. Pour batter onto crust. Bake at 350 degrees for 15 minutes.

REDUCE HEAT TO 200 DEGREES and bake for 2 hours, or until center is firm and no longer looks wet or shiny. Remove cake from oven and run a knife around inside edge of pan. Turn oven off and return cake to it for an additional 2 hours. Chill overnight.

lemon lime whipped cream

½ cup whipping cream
2 envelopes whipped topping mix
1 teaspoon lime peel, finely shredded
1 teaspoon lemon peel, finely shredded

In a small bowl, beat cream and whipped topping mix until stiff. Spread topping over cake. Decorate with shredded lime and lemon peels. Keep chilled.

MANDARIN ORANGE CHEESECAKE

Makes 12 slices

Bottoms up! This clever cheesecake is baked in a flan pan, inverted onto a serving plate, and decorated upside down. Your dessert companions will love it!

graham cracker crust

2 cups graham cracker crumbs

3 tablespoons sugar

⅓ teaspoon cinnamon

5 tablespoons butter or margarine, softened

In a small bowl, stir together crumbs, sugar, and cinnamon. Add melted butter and mix well. Press evenly onto bottom of greased 9-inch fluted flan pan. Set aside.

Have all ingredients at room temperature. Preheat oven to 350 degrees.

mandarin filling

24 ounces cream cheese

¾ cup sugar

3 tablespoons cornstarch

3 large eggs

1 egg yolk

2 teaspoons vanilla extract

1 tablespoon orange extract

½ cup frozen concentrated orange juice, thawed

11 ounce can mandarin orange segments, well drained

In a large bowl, beat cream cheese, sugar, and cornstarch with an electric mixer until smooth. Add eggs and yolk one at a time, beating well after each addition. Stir in vanilla and orange extracts and orange juice. Stir in orange segments. Pour cream cheese mixture onto crust. Bake at 350 degrees for 15 minutes.

i ♥ cheesecake

REDUCE HEAT TO 200 DEGREES and bake for 2 hours, or until center is firm and no longer looks wet or shiny. Remove cake from oven and carefully run a knife around inside edge of pan. Turn off oven and return cake to it for an additional 2 hours. Chill overnight.

topping
fresh fruit

Before serving, invert cheesecake onto a serving plate. Garnish top of graham cracker crust with fresh fruit. Keep chilled.

NEW ENGLAND APPLE CHEESECAKE

This is a New England treat!

Preheat oven to 350 degrees.

cheddar walnut cookie crust

¾ cup flour

2 tablespoons sugar

½ teaspoon cinnamon

1 egg, lightly beaten

¼ cup butter or margarine, softened

½ cup cheddar cheese, shredded

2 tablespoons walnuts, chopped

In a medium bowl, stir together flour, sugar, and cinnamon. Add egg and butter, beat with an electric mixer until well combined. Stir in shredded cheese and walnuts. With generously greased fingers, press cookie dough evenly onto bottom of greased 9-inch cheesecake pan. Bake 15–20 minutes or until golden.

Have all ingredients at room temperature. Keep oven at 350 degrees.

apple cheddar walnut filling

24 ounces cream cheese

¾ cup light brown sugar

3 tablespoons cornstarch

⅔ cup applesauce, sweetened or unsweetened, smooth or chunky

4 large eggs

¼ teaspoon cloves

2 teaspoons cinnamon

1 teaspoon nutmeg

1 cup cheddar cheese, shredded

¼ cup walnuts, chopped

i ♥ cheesecake

In a large bowl, beat cream cheese, brown sugar, cornstarch, and applesauce with an electric mixer until smooth. Add eggs one at a time, beating well after each addition. Stir in cloves, cinnamon, and nutmeg. Add shredded cheese and walnuts. Stir until well blended. Pour batter onto crust. Bake at 350 degrees for 15 minutes.

REDUCE HEAT TO 200 DEGREES and bake for 2 hours, or until center is firm and no longer looks wet or shiny. Remove cake from oven and run a knife around inside edge of pan. Turn oven off and return cake to it for an additional 2 hours. Chill overnight.

apple walnut topping

⅓ cup frozen concentrated apple juice, thawed
1 tablespoon light brown sugar
¼ teaspoon cinnamon
2 teaspoons cornstarch
2 tablespoons port wine
¼ cup walnuts, chopped

In a small heavy saucepan, stir together apple juice, brown sugar, cinnamon, cornstarch, and wine. Cook and stir over low heat until thickened and bubbly. Pour the topping over the cake while the topping is still warm. Sprinkle walnuts on top. Keep chilled.

PEACH PECAN CHEESECAKE

Makes 12–18 slices

This cheesecake combines fresh peaches and crunchy pecans for a scrumptious merger.

vanilla cookie crust

18 vanilla sandwich creme filled cookies, with fillings intact
5 tablespoons butter or margarine, melted
3 tablespoons pecans, chopped

Crush cookies to make crumbs. Place crumbs in a mixing bowl and add butter, mix well. Press crumb mixture evenly onto bottom of greased 9-inch cheesecake pan. Sprinkle pecans onto crust and set aside.

Have all ingredients at room temperature. Preheat oven to 350 degrees.

peach pecan filling

32 ounces cream cheese
1 cup dark brown sugar
3 tablespoons cornstarch
4 large eggs
2 teaspoons vanilla extract
1 teaspoon orange extract
¼ cup peach schnapps
1 cup fresh peaches, peeled and finely chopped
⅓ cup pecans, chopped

In a large bowl, beat cream cheese, brown sugar, and cornstarch with an electric mixer until smooth. Add eggs one at a time, beating well after each addition. Add vanilla and orange extracts. Stir in peach schnapps. Pour half of batter onto crust. Spoon on half of peaches and pecans. Pour remaining batter over peaches and pecans. Spoon on the rest of peaches and pecans. Bake at 350 degrees for 15 minutes.

i ♥ cheesecake

REDUCE HEAT TO 200 DEGREES and bake for 2 hours, or until center is firm and no longer looks wet or shiny. Remove cake from oven and run a knife around inside edge of pan. Turn oven off and return cake to it for an additional 2 hours. Chill overnight.

peach whipped cream

½ cup whipping cream
2 envelopes whipped topping mix
2 tablespoons dark brown sugar
2 teaspoons peach schnapps
3 tablespoons pecans, chopped

In a bowl, combine cream, whipped topping mix, brown sugar, and peach schnapps. Beat with an electric mixer until stiff. Spread whipped cream over the cake. Sprinkle with pecans. Keep chilled.

PEACHES 'N CREAM CHEESECAKE

Makes 12–18 slices

This rich cheesecake is bursting with fresh peaches. Choose peaches that are plump, somewhat firm, and have a creamy yellow color with a good pink blush.

graham cracker crust

2 cups graham cracker crumbs
5 tablespoons butter or margarine, melted
3 tablespoons sugar
¼ teaspoon cinnamon

Place crumbs in a mixing bowl and add butter, sugar, and cinnamon. Mix well. Press crumb mixture evenly onto bottom of greased 9-inch cheesecake pan. Set aside.

Have all ingredients at room temperature. Preheat oven to 350 degrees.

peachy cream filling

32 ounces cream cheese
1 cup sugar
3 tablespoons cornstarch
4 large eggs
2 teaspoons vanilla extract
1 teaspoon orange extract
1 cup fresh peaches, peeled and finely chopped

In a large bowl, beat cream cheese, sugar, and cornstarch with an electric mixer until smooth. Add eggs one at a time, beating well after each addition. Stir in vanilla and orange extracts. Stir in peaches. Pour batter onto crust. Without disturbing the crust, swirl the handle of a knife through the cake to separate peaches. Bake at 350 degrees for 15 minutes.

i ♥ cheesecake

REDUCE HEAT TO 200 DEGREES and bake for 2 hours, or until center is firm and no longer looks wet or shiny. Remove cake from oven and run a knife around inside edge of pan. Turn oven off and return cake to it for an additional 2 hours. Chill overnight.

warm peach topping

2 medium peaches, sliced
1 tablespoon lemon juice
1 cup peach preserves

In a medium bowl, toss together peaches and lemon juice. Drain juice from bowl. Arrange slices on top of cheesecake. Chill until serving time. Immediately before serving, in a small saucepan, heat peach preserves. Drizzle warm preserves over cake. Keep chilled.

PEAR ELEGANCE CHEESECAKE

Makes 12–18 slices

A chocolate cookie crust, fresh pear filling, and easy pear glaze give this cheesecake an air of elegance.

chocolate cookie crust

18 chocolate sandwich creme filled cookies, with fillings intact
5 tablespoons butter or margarine, melted

Crush cookies to make crumbs and add butter, mix well. Press cookie mixture evenly onto bottom of greased 9-inch cheesecake pan. Set aside.

Have all ingredients at room temperature. Preheat oven to 350 degrees.

pear filling

32 ounces cream cheese
1 cup sugar
3 tablespoons cornstarch
4 large eggs
⅔ cup pureed pear (1 medium pear)
½ cup pear schnapps
2 teaspoons vanilla extract
1 teaspoon lemon extract
1½ teaspoons orange extract

In a large bowl, beat cream cheese, sugar, and cornstarch with an electric mixer until smooth. Add eggs one at a time, beating well after each addition. Stir in pureed pear, pear schnapps, and vanilla, lemon, and orange extracts. Pour batter onto crust. Bake at 350 degrees for 15 minutes.

REDUCE HEAT TO 200 DEGREES and bake for 2 hours, or until center is firm and no longer looks wet or shiny. Remove cake from oven and run a knife around inside edge of pan. Turn oven off and return cake to it for an additional 2 hours. Chill overnight.

i ♥ cheesecake

pear glaze

½ cup pear preserves
½ cup orange marmalade
½ medium pear, sliced
2 teaspoons lemon juice

In a small heavy saucepan, stir together pear preserves and orange marmalade. Cook and stir until heated through. Pour over cheesecake. Dip pear slices in lemon juice. Arrange pear slices over cake. Chill until serving time.

RASPBERRY ALMOND CHEESECAKE

Fresh raspberries are at their peak from July through September. For best results, use within 24 hours after buying.

vanilla cookie crust

18 vanilla sandwich creme filled cookies, with fillings intact
3 tablespoons almonds, toasted and coarsely chopped
5 tablespoons butter or margarine, melted

Crush cookies to make crumbs. Place crumbs in a mixing bowl then add almonds and butter. Mix well. Press crumb mixture evenly onto bottom of greased 9-inch cheesecake pan. Set aside.

Have all ingredients at room temperature. Preheat oven to 350 degrees.

raspberry filling

32 ounces cream cheese
1 cup sugar
3 tablespoons cornstarch
¼ cup sour cream
⅓ cup raspberry schnapps
4 large eggs
2 teaspoons almond extract
2 teaspoons vanilla extract
½ teaspoon lemon extract
½ teaspoon cinnamon
⅔ cup fresh or frozen raspberries; if using frozen, thaw and drain well
¼ cup almonds, toasted and coarsely chopped

In a large bowl, beat cream cheese, sugar, cornstarch, sour cream, and raspberry schnapps with an electric mixer until smooth. Add eggs one at a time, beating well after each addition. Stir in almond,

i ♥ cheesecake

vanilla, and lemon extracts and cinnamon. Carefully stir in raspberries and almonds. Pour batter onto crust. Bake at 350 degrees for 15 minutes.

REDUCE HEAT TO 200 DEGREES and bake for 2 hours, or until center is firm and no longer looks wet or shiny. Remove cake from oven and carefully run a knife around inside edge of pan. Turn oven off and return cake to it for an additional 2 hours. Chill overnight.

fresh raspberry whipped cream

1 cup whipping cream
1 tablespoon sugar
fresh raspberries
3 tablespoons almonds, toasted and coarsely chopped

In a small bowl, beat whipping cream and sugar with an electric mixer until stiff. Pipe whipped cream around edge of cheesecake. Garnish with raspberries and almonds. Keep chilled.

RASPBERRY CHOCOLATE CHEESECAKE

chocolate cookie crust

18 chocolate creme filled cookies, with fillings intact
3 tablespoon almonds, toasted and coarsely chopped
5 tablespoons butter or margarine, melted

Crush cookies to make crumbs. Place crumbs in a mixing bowl, add almonds and butter, mix well. Press crumb mixture evenly onto bottom of greased 9-inch cheesecake pan. Set aside.

Have all ingredients at room temperature. Preheat oven to 350 degrees.

fresh raspberry filling

32 ounces cream cheese
1 cup sugar
3 tablespoons cornstarch
½ cup sour cream
4 large eggs
1 teaspoon almond extract
1 teaspoon vanilla extract
½ teaspoon lemon extract
½ teaspoon cinnamon
¾ cup fresh or frozen raspberries; if using frozen, thaw and drain well

In a large bowl, beat cream cheese, sugar, cornstarch, and sour cream with an electric mixer until smooth. Add eggs one at a time, beating well after each addition. Stir in almond, vanilla, and lemon extracts and cinnamon. Stir in raspberries, mix well. Pour batter onto crust. Bake at 350 degrees for 15 minutes.

i ♥ cheesecake

REDUCE HEAT TO 200 DEGREES and bake for 2 hours, or until center is firm and no longer looks wet or shiny. Remove cake from oven and carefully run a knife around inside edge of pan. Turn oven off and return cake to it for an additional 2 hours. Chill overnight.

chocolate raspberry topping

3 ounces semisweet chocolate chips
¼ cup raspberry preserves, jelly, or jam
fresh raspberries
3 tablespoon almonds, toasted and coarsely chopped

In a small heavy saucepan, combine chocolate chips and raspberry preserves. Stir constantly over low heat while melting chocolate until mixture is smooth. Spread warm mixture over top of cheesecake. Decorate with raspberries and almonds. Keep chilled.

STRAWBERRY CHEESECAKE

Makes 12–18 slices

America's favorite berry tastes great in this easy cheesecake. Be sure to buy enough fresh berries for the filling and topping.

graham cracker crust

2 cups graham cracker crumbs

3 tablespoons sugar

5 tablespoons butter or margarine, melted

Place crumbs in a mixing bowl, add sugar and butter, mix well. Press crumb mixture evenly onto bottom of greased 9-inch cheesecake pan. Set aside.

Have all ingredients at room temperature. Preheat oven to 350 degrees.

strawberry filling

24 ounces cream cheese

1 cup sugar

3 tablespoons cornstarch

4 large eggs

1 tablespoon lemon juice

2 teaspoons vanilla extract

2 teaspoons strawberry flavoring

2 drops red food coloring

1¼ cups fresh strawberries, washed, hulled, and sliced

In a large bowl, beat cream cheese, sugar, and cornstarch with an electric mixer until smooth. Add eggs one at a time, beating well after each addition. Stir in lemon juice, vanilla extract, strawberry flavoring, and food coloring. Stir in strawberries. Pour batter onto crust. Bake at 350 degrees for 15 minutes.

i ♥ cheesecake

REDUCE HEAT TO 200 DEGREES and bake for 2 hours, or until center is firm and no longer looks wet or shiny. Remove cake from oven and carefully run a knife around inside edge of pan. Turn oven off and return cake to it for an additional 2 hours. Chill overnight.

creamy white topping

½ cup shortening
1 teaspoon almond extract
3 cups sifted powdered sugar
1½ to 2 tablespoons milk
fresh strawberries

In a medium bowl, beat shortening and almond extract with an electric mixer until smooth. Slowly add half of the powdered sugar, beating well. Add 1 tablespoon milk. Gradually beat in remaining powdered sugar. Add enough of the remaining milk to make a spreading consistency. Spread topping over cheesecake. Garnish with strawberries. Chill until serving time.

STRAWBERRY SUNDAE CHEESECAKE

chocolate-covered strawberries (for topping)

Melt 4 ounces semisweet chocolate over low heat, stirring constantly. Spoon chocolate over 12 whole strawberries and place on baking sheet lined with waxed paper. Chill until chocolate hardens.

chocolate cookie crust

18 chocolate sandwich creme filled cookies, with fillings intact
5 tablespoons butter or margarine, melted

Crush cookies to make crumbs. Place crumbs in a mixing bowl and add butter, mix well. Press crumb mixture evenly onto bottom of greased 9-inch cheesecake pan. Set aside.

Have all ingredients at room temperature. Preheat oven to 350 degrees.

strawberry chocolate filling

32 ounces cream cheese
1 cup sugar
3 tablespoons cornstarch
4 large eggs
2 teaspoons vanilla extract
2 tablespoons cocoa powder
3 tablespoons powdered sugar
12 ounces frozen strawberries (juice and berries), thawed
2 teaspoons strawberry flavoring
½ teaspoon lemon extract

In a large bowl, beat cream cheese, sugar, and cornstarch with an electric mixer until smooth. Add eggs one at a time, beating well after each addition. Stir in vanilla extract. Remove ¾ cup of mixture

i ♥ cheesecake

and put in a small bowl. To this mixture, add cocoa and powdered sugar, mix well. Set aside. To original mixture, stir in strawberries and juice. Stir in strawberry flavoring and lemon extract. Pour half of original mixture onto crust. Spoon on half of cocoa mixture. Pour remainder of original mixture on top of cocoa mixture. Spoon on remaining cocoa mixture. Without disturbing crust, swirl the handle of a knife through cake, creating a marbling effect. Bake at 350 degrees for 15 minutes.

REDUCE HEAT TO 200 DEGREES and bake for 2 hours, or until center is firm and no longer looks wet or shiny. Remove cake from oven and run a knife around inside edge of pan. Turn oven off and return cake to it for an additional 2 hours. Chill overnight.

easy whipped cream topping

2 tablespoons powdered sugar
1 tablespoon cocoa
1 cup whipping cream
12 chocolate-covered strawberries

In a small bowl, combine powdered sugar and cocoa. Stir in cream and beat until stiff. Spread cream on top of cake or pipe around edge of cake. Decorate with chocolate-covered strawberries. Keep chilled.

TANGERINE CHEESECAKE

vanilla cookie crust

18 vanilla sandwich creme filled cookies, with fillings intact
5 tablespoons butter or margarine, melted

Crush cookies to make crumbs. Place crumbs in a mixing bowl and add butter, mix well. Press crumb mixture evenly onto bottom of greased 9-inch cheesecake pan. Set aside.

Have all ingredients at room temperature. Preheat oven to 350 degrees.

Look for fresh tangerines from November to May, and choose ones that are heavy and firm with fairly tight skin.

tangerine filling

32 ounces cream cheese
1 cup sugar
3 tablespoons cornstarch
4 large eggs
1 teaspoon vanilla extract
¾ teaspoon lemon extract
2 teaspoons orange extract
⅔ cup frozen tangerine juice concentrate, thawed
2 drops orange food coloring
1 tangerine, peeled, seeded, and separated into segments

In a large bowl, beat cream cheese, sugar, and cornstarch with an electric mixer until smooth. Add eggs one at a time, beating well after each addition. Stir in vanilla, lemon, and orange extracts. Stir in tangerine juice, food coloring, and tangerine segments. Pour batter onto crust. Bake at 350 degrees for 15 minutes.

i ♥ cheesecake

REDUCE HEAT TO 200 DEGREES and bake for 2 hours, or until center is firm and no longer looks wet or shiny. Remove cake from oven and carefully run a knife around inside edge of pan. Turn oven off and return cake to it for an additional 2 hours. Chill overnight.

white chocolate marmalade topping

5 ounces white chocolate

⅓ cup orange marmalade

1 teaspoon orange extract

1 tangerine, peeled, seeded, and separated into segments

In a small heavy saucepan, melt chocolate over low heat while stirring constantly until melted and smooth. Stir in marmalade and orange extract. Spread warm topping on cake. Garnish with tangerine segments. Keep chilled.

notes

mint

CHOCOLATE MINT CHEESECAKE	198
MINT ALMOND SWIRL CHEESECAKE	200
PEPPERMINT CHIP CHEESECAKE	202

CHOCOLATE MINT CHEESECAKE

This colorful cheesecake has three layers marbled together.

chocolate cookie crust

18 chocolate sandwich creme filled cookies, with fillings intact
5 tablespoons butter or margarine, melted

Crush cookies to make crumbs. Place crumbs in a mixing bowl and add butter, mix well. Press crumb mixture evenly onto bottom of greased 9-inch cheesecake pan. Set aside.

Have all ingredients at room temperature. Preheat oven to 350 degrees.

chocolate mint filling

32 ounces cream cheese
1 cup sugar
3 tablespoons cornstarch
4 large eggs
⅓ cup crème de menthe
⅓ cup crème de cacao
2 teaspoons vanilla extract

In a large bowl, beat cream cheese, sugar, and cornstarch with an electric mixer until smooth. Add eggs one at a time, beating well after each addition. Add crème de menthe, crème de cacao, and vanilla extract. Mix thoroughly. Pour filling onto crust. Bake at 350 degrees for 15 minutes.

REDUCE HEAT TO 200 DEGREES and bake for 2 hours, or until center is firm and no longer looks wet or shiny. Remove cake from oven and run a knife around inside edge of pan. Turn oven off and return cake to it for an additional 2 hours. Chill overnight.

i ♥ cheesecake

mint whipped cream

1 cup whipping cream
1 envelope whipped topping mix
1 tablespoon crème de menthe
chocolate ice cream topping (the type that forms a hardened shell)

In a small bowl, beat cream, whipped topping mix, and crème de menthe until thickened. Spread whipped cream on cake. Drizzle chocolate topping over top. Keep chilled.

MINT ALMOND SWIRL CHEESECAKE

Makes 12–18 slices

Crème de menthe liqueur and Amaretto team up to enliven this luscious dessert cake.

chocolate cookie crust

18 chocolate mint sandwich creme filled cookies, with fillings intact
5 tablespoons butter or margarine, melted
3 tablespoons almonds, chopped

Crush cookies to make crumbs. Place crumbs in a mixing bowl and add butter, mix well. Press crumb mixture evenly onto bottom of greased 9-inch cheesecake pan. Sprinkle with chopped almonds.

Have all ingredients at room temperature. Preheat oven to 350 degrees.

mint almond filling

32 ounces cream cheese
1 cup sugar
3 tablespoons cornstarch
2 teaspoons vanilla extract
4 large eggs
⅓ cup crème de menthe
⅓ cup Amaretto

In a large bowl, beat cream cheese, sugar, cornstarch, and vanilla extract with an electric mixer until smooth. Add eggs one at a time, beating well after each addition. Remove half of mixture and put into a medium bowl. To this mixture, add crème de menthe, mixing thoroughly. Set aside. To original mixture, add Amaretto, mix thoroughly. Pour crème de menthe mixture onto crust. Spoon on Amaretto mixture, carefully spreading it out and making it the second layer. Without disturbing the crust, carefully swirl the handle of a knife through the batter a couple of times. Bake at 350 degrees for 15 minutes.

i ♥ cheesecake

REDUCE HEAT TO 200 DEGREES and bake for 2 hours, or until center is firm and no longer looks wet or shiny. Remove cake from oven and run a knife around inside edge of pan. Turn oven off and return cake to it for an additional 2 hours. Chill overnight.

chocolate mint topping

6 ounces mint chocolate chips
⅓ cup sour cream
2 teaspoons crème de menthe
3 tablespoons almonds, chopped

In a small heavy saucepan, combine chocolate chips, sour cream, and crème de menthe. Stir constantly while melting the chocolate on low heat. Spread topping over cake. Sprinkle with chopped almonds. Keep chilled.

PEPPERMINT CHIP CHEESECAKE

Romance your guest by making individual heart-shaped cheesecakes. Simply use 4-inch heart-shaped tart pans instead of a 9-inch pan and bake at 200 degrees for 35 to 45 minutes.

chocolate mint cookie crust

18 chocolate mint sandwich creme filled cookies, with fillings intact
5 tablespoons butter or margarine, melted

Crush cookies to make crumbs. Place crumbs in a mixing bowl and add butter, mix well. Press crumb mixture evenly onto bottom of greased 9-inch cheesecake pan. Set aside.

Have all ingredients at room temperature. Preheat oven to 350 degrees.

chocolate mint filling

32 ounces cream cheese
1 cup sugar
3 tablespoons cornstarch
4 large eggs
½ cup sour cream
2 teaspoons vanilla extract
2 teaspoons peppermint extract
⅓ cup peppermint schnapps
2 drops red food coloring
1 cup mint flavored chocolate chips

In a large bowl, beat cream cheese, sugar, and cornstarch with an electric mixer until smooth. Add eggs one at a time, beating well after each addition. Stir in sour cream and vanilla and peppermint extracts. Stir in peppermint schnapps. Remove ½ cup of mixture. To this mixture, add red food coloring. Blend well and set aside. To original mixture, add chocolate chips. Pour half of original mixture onto crust. Pour on half of colored mixture. Pour rest of original mixture on top of colored. Pour

i ♥ cheesecake

on rest of colored mixture. Without disturbing crust, swirl the handle of a knife through cake, creating a marbling effect. Bake at 350 degrees for 15 minutes.

REDUCE HEAT TO 200 DEGREES and bake for 2 hours, or until center is firm and no longer looks wet or shiny. Remove cake from oven and run a knife around inside edge of pan. Turn oven off and return cake to it for an additional 2 hours. Chill overnight.

white chocolate glaze

12 ounces white chocolate
2 tablespoons whipping cream
3 ounces semisweet chocolate chips
1 tablespoon butter or margarine

In a small heavy saucepan, melt white chocolate over low heat, stirring constantly. Stir in whipping cream. Spread white chocolate mixture over cheesecake. Chill. In a small heavy saucepan, melt semisweet chocolate and butter over low heat, stirring constantly. Drizzle over white chocolate mixture. Chill until serving time.

notes

nut

ALMOND COFFEE SWIRL CHEESECAKE

mocha cookie crust

2 cups chocolate wafers

5 tablespoons butter or margarine, melted

2 teaspoons instant coffee, dissolved in 2 teaspoons boiling water

3 tablespoons almonds, chopped

Crush cookies to make crumbs. Place crumbs in a mixing bowl and add butter and coffee mixture, mixing well. Press crumb mixture evenly onto bottom of greased 9-inch cheesecake pan. Sprinkle with almonds. Set aside.

Have all ingredients at room temperature. Preheat oven to 350 degrees.

amaretto coffee filling

24 ounces cream cheese

¾ cup sugar

3 tablespoons cornstarch

4 large eggs

1 egg yolk

¼ cup coffee flavored liqueur

1 teaspoon instant coffee, dissolved in 1 teaspoon boiling water

¼ cup Amaretto

½ teaspoon almond extract

In a large bowl, beat cream cheese, sugar, and cornstarch using an electric mixer until smooth. Add eggs and yolk one at a time, beating well after each addition. Remove half of batter and place it in a medium bowl. To batter in large bowl, stir in coffee liqueur and dissolved instant coffee. Stir Amaretto and almond extract into batter in medium bowl. Pour coffee mixture onto crust. Spoon on

Amaretto mixture and carefully spread it out, making it the second layer. Without disturbing the crust, carefully swirl the handle of a knife through the batter a couple of times. Bake at 350 degrees for 15 minutes.

REDUCE HEAT TO 200 DEGREES and bake for 2 hours, or until center is firm and no longer looks wet or shiny. Remove cake from oven and run a knife around inside edge of pan. Turn oven off and return cake to it for an additional 2 hours. Chill overnight.

coffee whipped cream
⅔ cup whipping cream
3 tablespoons powdered sugar
1 teaspoon instant coffee, dissolved in 1 teaspoon boiling water
½ teaspoon vanilla extract
3 tablespoons almonds, chopped

In a small bowl, beat cream, powdered sugar, dissolved instant coffee, and vanilla extract with an electric mixer until thickened. Spread whipped topping onto cake, creating a design by drawing swirls with bottom of a spoon. Sprinkle with almonds. Keep chilled.

BAKLAVA CHEESECAKE

Phyllo dough is used for the crust in this Middle Eastern–inspired cheesecake. Look for it in your grocer's freezer case.

phyllo crust

3 sheets frozen phyllo dough, thawed
3 tablespoons butter or margarine, melted

Place 1 sheet of phyllo on bottom of greased 9-inch cheesecake pan, folding to fit. Brush dough with some of butter. Repeat layering and brushing with remaining phyllo dough and butter. Cover top of pan with plastic wrap or a damp kitchen towel. Set aside.

Have all ingredients at room temperature. Preheat oven to 350 degrees.

double nut, coconut filling

24 ounces cream cheese
⅔ cup sugar
¼ cup honey
2 tablespoons rose water or rose syrup (this can be found in a Middle Eastern food store)
3 tablespoons cornstarch
4 large eggs
1 teaspoon lemon peel, finely shredded
2 tablespoons almonds, coarsely chopped
⅓ cup walnuts, coarsely chopped
¼ cup coconut, flaked or freshly grated

In a large bowl, combine cream cheese, sugar, honey, rose water, and cornstarch with an electric mixer until smooth. Add eggs one at a time, beating well after each addition. Stir in lemon peel, almonds, walnuts, and coconut. Pour filling onto crust. Bake at 350 degrees for 15 minutes.

i ♥ cheesecake

REDUCE HEAT TO 200 DEGREES and bake for 2 hours, or until center is firm and no longer looks wet or shiny. Remove cake from oven and carefully run a knife around inside edge of pan. Turn oven off and return cake to it for an additional 2 hours. Chill overnight.

nutty coconut topping

⅓ cup sugar

¼ cup water

1 tablespoon honey

2 teaspoons cornstarch

1 teaspoon rose water or rose syrup

½ cup coconut, flaked or freshly grated

2 tablespoons almonds, coarsely chopped

¼ cup walnuts, coarsely chopped

In a small heavy saucepan, cook and stir sugar, water, honey, cornstarch, and rose water until sugar dissolves. Bring to a boil, then simmer for about 20 minutes, stirring occasionally until thickened. Stir in coconut, almonds, and walnuts. Spread warm syrup on cake. Keep chilled.

CALIFORNIA AMARETTO CHEESECAKE

chocolate cookie crust

18 chocolate sandwich creme filled cookie, with fillings intact
5 tablespoons butter or margarine, melted
3 tablespoons whole almonds

Californians love to combine the flavors of almonds, orange, and chocolate.

Crush cookies to make crumbs. Place crumbs in a mixing bowl and add butter and nuts, mix well. Press crumb mixture evenly onto bottom of greased 9-inch cheesecake pan. Set aside.

Have all ingredients at room temperature. Preheat oven to 350 degrees.

amaretto, orange, and almond filling

24 ounces cream cheese
⅔ cup sugar
3 tablespoons cornstarch
3 large eggs
1 egg yolk
½ cup Amaretto
2 teaspoons almond extract
¾ teaspoon lemon extract
1¼ teaspoons orange extract
4 tablespoons whole almonds

In a large bowl, beat cream cheese, sugar, and cornstarch with an electric mixer until smooth. Add eggs and yolk one at a time, beating well after each addition. Stir in Amaretto and almond, lemon, and orange extracts. Stir until well blended. Stir in almonds. Pour filling onto crust. Bake at 350 degrees for 15 minutes.

i ♥ cheesecake

REDUCE HEAT TO 200 DEGREES and bake for 2 hours, or until center is firm and no longer looks wet or shiny. Remove cake from oven and carefully run a knife around inside edge of pan. Turn oven off and return cake to it for an additional 2 hours. Chill overnight.

orange marmalade and almond topping

2 ounces frozen concentrated orange juice, thawed
⅓ cup orange marmalade
4 teaspoons cornstarch
2 teaspoons lemon juice
½ teaspoon almond extract
3 tablespoons almonds, chopped
whole almonds
part of a sliced orange
chocolate ice cream topping (the type that forms a hardened shell)

In a small heavy saucepan, combine orange juice, marmalade, and cornstarch. Cook and stir over low heat until thickened. Remove from heat and stir in lemon juice and almond extract. Put topping on cake while topping is still warm. Sprinkle with chopped almonds. Decorate with whole almonds and sliced orange. Drizzle with chocolate topping. Keep chilled.

MAPLE PECAN CHEESECAKE

Makes 12–18 slices

vanilla cookie crust

18 vanilla sandwich creme filled cookies, with fillings intact
5 tablespoons butter or margarine, softened

Crush cookies to make crumbs. Place crumbs in a mixing bowl and add butter, mix well. Press crumb mixture evenly onto bottom of greased 9-inch cheesecake pan. Set aside.

For a real treat, use real maple syrup.

Have all ingredients at room temperature. Preheat oven to 350 degrees.

maple pecan filling

24 ounces cream cheese
¾ cup light brown sugar
⅓ cup maple syrup
3 tablespoons cornstarch
3 large eggs
1 egg yolk
2 teaspoons vanilla extract
1½ teaspoons butter flavoring
⅔ cup pecans, coarsely chopped

In a large bowl, beat cream cheese, brown sugar, maple syrup, and cornstarch with an electric mixer until smooth. Add eggs and yolk one at a time, beating well after each addition. Stir in vanilla extract and butter flavoring. Stir in chopped pecans. Pour filling onto crust. Bake at 350 degrees for 15 minutes.

REDUCE HEAT TO 200 DEGREES and bake for 2 hours, or until center is firm and no longer looks wet or shiny. Remove cake from oven and carefully run a knife around inside edge of pan. Turn oven off and return cake to it for an additional 2 hours. Chill overnight.

whipped cream topping

⅔ cup whipping cream
2 envelopes whipped topping mix
1 teaspoon maple flavoring
¼ cup pecans, coarsely chopped

In a bowl, combine cream, whipped topping mix, and maple flavoring. Beat until stiff. Spread whipped cream on cake, creating a design by drawing swirls with bottom of a spoon. Sprinkle with pecans. Keep chilled.

notes

peanut butter

PEANUT BUTTER AND BANANA CHEESECAKE   216

PEANUT BUTTER AND CHOCOLATE CHEESECAKE   218

PEANUT BUTTER AND JELLY CHEESECAKE   220

PEANUT BUTTER AND BANANA CHEESECAKE

This is for those of us who relish peanut butter and banana sandwiches. Here's a delicious dessert to satisfy our cravings.

peanut butter cookie crust

18 peanut butter sandwich creme filled cookies, with fillings intact
3 tablespoons peanuts, chopped
5 tablespoons butter or margarine, melted

Crush cookies to make crumbs. Place crumbs in a mixing bowl and add peanuts and butter, mix well. Press crumb mixture evenly onto bottom of greased 9-inch cheesecake pan. Set aside.

Have all ingredients at room temperature. Preheat oven to 350 degrees.

peanut butter and banana filling

32 ounces cream cheese
¾ cup dark brown sugar
3 tablespoons cornstarch
2 teaspoons vanilla extract
4 large eggs
½ cup mashed banana (1 small banana)
1 tablespoon banana flavoring
¾ cup creamy peanut butter
⅓ cup peanuts, chopped

In a large bowl, beat cream cheese, brown sugar, and cornstarch with an electric mixer until smooth. Stir in vanilla extract. Add eggs one at a time, beating well after each addition. Remove ⅔ cup of mixture and put into a small bowl. To this mixture, add mashed banana and banana flavoring, mixing well. Set aside. To the original mixture, add peanut butter, mix thoroughly. Stir in the chopped peanuts. Pour half of original mixture onto crust. Spoon on banana mixture, spreading this out and

i ♥ cheesecake

making it the second layer. Pour the rest of original mixture on top of banana mixture, spreading it out also. Bake at 350 degrees for 15 minutes.

REDUCE HEAT TO 200 DEGREES and bake for 2 hours, or until center is firm and no longer looks wet or shiny. Remove cake from oven and run a knife around inside edge of pan. Turn oven off and return cake to it for an additional 2 hours. Chill overnight.

chocolate peanut butter topping

6 ounces white chocolate
½ cup creamy peanut butter
3 tablespoons peanuts, chopped

In small heavy saucepan, melt chocolate over low heat, stirring constantly. Remove from heat and stir in peanut butter. Spread topping on cake and sprinkle with peanuts. Keep chilled.

PEANUT BUTTER AND CHOCOLATE CHEESECAKE

Attention all peanut butter and chocolate addicts: you'll go wild over this decadent cheesecake.

chocolate peanut butter crust

1 cup chocolate wafers, finely crushed
1 cup crisp peanut butter cookies, finely crushed
¼ cup peanuts, finely chopped
½ cup butter or margarine, melted

Place crushed chocolate wafers, crushed peanut butter cookies, and chopped peanuts in a medium bowl and add butter. Mix thoroughly. Press crumb mixture evenly onto bottom and up the sides of greased 9-inch cheesecake pan. Set aside.

Have all ingredients at room temperature. Preheat oven to 350 degrees.

peanut butter and chocolate filling

32 ounces cream cheese
1 cup dark brown sugar
3 tablespoons cornstarch
½ cup sour cream
5 large eggs
2 teaspoons vanilla extract
¾ cup creamy peanut butter
1 cup semisweet chocolate chips, melted
⅔ cup peanuts, chopped

In a large bowl, beat cream cheese, brown sugar, cornstarch, and sour cream with an electric mixer until smooth. Add eggs one at a time, beating well after each addition. Add vanilla extract and peanut

i ♥ cheesecake

butter, blend thoroughly. Stir in melted chocolate chips, mixing thoroughly. Stir in chopped peanuts, mixing thoroughly. Bake at 350 degrees for 15 minutes.

REDUCE HEAT TO 200 DEGREES and bake for 2 hours, or until center is firm and no longer looks wet or shiny. Remove cake from oven and run a knife around inside edge of pan. Turn oven off and return cake to it for an additional 2 hours. Chill overnight.

peanut butter and chocolate swirl topping

8 ounces white chocolate chips
2 tablespoons creamy peanut butter
1 ounce semisweet chocolate, melted

In a small heavy saucepan, melt white chocolate and peanut butter over low heat, stirring constantly. Cool to luke warm. Pour peanut butter mixture over cheesecake. Drizzle parallel strips of semisweet chocolate over peanut butter mixture. To decorate, draw the dull side of the tip of a knife across the chocolate strips. Chill until serving time.

PEANUT BUTTER AND JELLY CHEESECAKE

It's better than the sandwich!

peanut butter cookie crust

18 peanut butter sandwich creme filled cookies, with fillings intact
3 tablespoons peanuts, chopped
5 tablespoons butter or margarine, melted

Crush cookies to make crumbs. Place crumbs and peanuts in mixing bowl and add butter, mix well. Press crumb mixture evenly onto bottom of greased 9-inch cheesecake pan. Set aside.

Have all ingredients at room temperature. Preheat oven to 350 degrees.

peanut butter filling

32 ounces cream cheese
¾ cup dark brown sugar
¾ cup sour cream
2 teaspoons vanilla extract
4 large eggs
1 cup creamy peanut butter
⅔ cup peanuts, chopped

In a large bowl, beat cream cheese, brown sugar, and sour cream with an electric mixer until smooth. Stir in vanilla extract. Add eggs one at a time, beating well after each addition. Stir in peanut butter, mixing thoroughly. Stir in chopped peanuts. Pour filling onto crust. Bake at 350 degrees for 15 minutes.

REDUCE HEAT TO 200 DEGREES and bake for 2 hours, or until center is firm and no longer looks wet or shiny. Remove cake from oven and run a knife around inside edge of pan. Turn oven off and return cake to it for an additional 2 hours. Chill overnight.

i ♥ cheesecake

easy jelly topping

1 cup strawberry preserves

In a small heavy saucepan, heat preserves until warm and smooth. Spread over top of cheesecake. Chill until serving time.

notes

vanilla

HONEY VANILLA CHEESECAKE

This cheesecake has a dose of honey in it.

chocolate cookie crust

18 chocolate sandwich creme filled cookies, with fillings intact
5 tablespoons butter or margarine, melted

Crush cookies to make crumbs. Place crumbs in medium bowl and add butter, mix well. Press crust evenly onto bottom of greased 9-inch cheesecake pan. Set aside.

Have all ingredients at room temperature. Preheat oven to 350 degrees.

creamy honey almond filling

32 ounces cream cheese
1 cup sugar
¼ cup honey
3 tablespoons cornstarch
¾ cup whipping cream
4 large eggs
¼ cup vanilla extract
2 teaspoons almond extract
½ cup almonds, toasted and chopped

In a large bowl, beat cream cheese, sugar, honey, cornstarch, and cream with an electric mixer until smooth. Add eggs one at a time, beating well after each addition. Stir in vanilla and almond extracts and almonds, mixing thoroughly. Pour filling onto crust. Bake at 350 degrees for 15 minutes.

REDUCE HEAT TO 200 DEGREES and bake for 2 hours, or until center is firm and no longer looks wet or shiny. Remove cake from oven and carefully run a knife around inside edge of pan. Turn oven off and return cake to it for an additional 2 hours. Chill overnight.

easy vanilla topping

1 cup whipping cream
1 teaspoon vanilla extract
2 tablespoons powdered sugar

Place whipping cream, vanilla extract, and powdered sugar in medium bowl. Beat with an electric mixer until cream is thickened and holds stiff peaks. Spread cream over top of cheesecake. Keep chilled.

INDIVIDUAL CHEESECAKES

vanilla wafer crust

30 vanilla wafers

Place 2½-inch cupcake liner in each compartment of cupcake pan(s). Place one vanilla wafer in each, flat side down.

Have all ingredients at room temperature. Preheat oven to 200 degrees.

creamy orange filling

32 ounces cream cheese
1 cup sugar
3 tablespoons cornstarch
4 large eggs
2¼ teaspoons orange extract
2 teaspoons vanilla extract
1¼ teaspoons lemon extract
½ cup sour cream

In a large bowl, beat cream cheese, sugar, and cornstarch with an electric mixer until smooth. Add eggs one at a time, beating well after each addition. Add orange, vanilla, and lemon extracts. Stir in sour cream. Mix well without overbeating. Put ¼ cup (4 tablespoons) in each liner. Bake at 200 degrees for 35 to 45 minutes, or until done—the cupcakes will spring back if touched when done. Remove cupcakes from oven and cool in muffin pan to room temperature. Chill overnight.

whipped cream topping

1 cup whipping cream
3 tablespoons powdered sugar

i ♥ cheesecake

1 teaspoon vanilla extract

1 teaspoon orange extract

½ teaspoon lemon extract

In a small bowl, beat cream and powdered sugar until mixture starts to thicken. Add vanilla, orange, and lemon extracts and beat until stiff. Spread whipped cream over cupcakes. Keep chilled.

orange glaze

1 cup orange marmalade

1 tablespoon cornstarch

2 teaspoons lemon juice

1 teaspoon orange extract

⅓ cup pecans or walnuts, chopped

In a small heavy saucepan, combine marmalade, cornstarch, lemon juice, and orange extract. Cook and stir over low heat until thickened—about 2 minutes. Spread over cupcakes while glaze is still warm. Sprinkle with chopped nuts. Keep chilled.

SUPER NEW YORK STYLE CHEESECAKE

Preheat oven to 350 degrees.

homemade cookie crust

1 cup flour
⅓ cup sugar
2 eggs, lightly beaten
⅓ cup butter or margarine, softened
1 teaspoon vanilla extract

Mix flour and sugar. Add eggs, butter, and vanilla extract. Mix well. With generously greased fingers, press dough evenly onto bottom of greased 9-inch cheesecake pan. Bake 12–15 minutes or until lightly browned.

slice-and-bake cookie crust

Use 8 ounces of a roll of slice-and-bake refrigerated sugar cookie dough. Slice as you would to make cookies. With generously greased fingers, arrange in circles, starting on the outside edge of the pan and working your way in on the bottom of the pan. With fingertips, press dough evenly onto the bottom of the pan as if to make one big cookie. Bake 15–17 minutes or until lightly browned. Remove from oven and set aside.

Have all ingredients at room temperature. Keep oven at 350 degrees.

new york filling

40 ounces cream cheese
1½ cups sugar
3 tablespoons cornstarch
5 large eggs

i ♥ cheesecake

1 tablespoon vanilla extract
2¼ teaspoons orange extract
1½ teaspoons lemon extract
1 cup whipping cream

In a large bowl, beat cream cheese, sugar, and cornstarch with an electric mixer until smooth. Add eggs one at a time, beating well after each addition. Stir in vanilla, orange, and lemon extracts. Stir in cream. Pour filling onto crust. Bake at 350 degrees for 15 minutes.

REDUCE HEAT TO 200 DEGREES and bake for 2 hours, or until center is firm and no longer looks wet or shiny. Remove cake from oven and carefully run a knife around inside edge of pan. Turn oven off and return cake to it for an additional 2 hours. Chill overnight.

whipped cream topping

⅔ cup whipping cream
2 envelopes whipped topping mix

In a bowl, beat cream and whipped topping mix until stiff. Spread cream over cake.

orange glaze

5 ounces white chocolate
⅓ cup orange marmalade
1 teaspoon orange extract
½ cup pecans or walnuts, chopped

In a small heavy saucepan, combine chocolate, marmalade, and orange extract. Cook and stir over low heat until chocolate is melted and mixture is smooth. Spread over cake while glaze is still warm. Sprinkle with chopped nuts. Keep chilled.

VANILLA SUPREME CHEESECAKE

vanilla cookie crust

18 vanilla sandwich creme filled cookies, with fillings intact
5 tablespoons butter or margarine, melted

Crush cookies to make crumbs. Place crumbs in a mixing bowl and add butter, mix well. Press crumb mixture evenly onto bottom of greased 9-inch cheesecake pan. Set aside.

Have all ingredients at room temperature. Preheat oven to 350 degrees.

supreme vanilla filling

32 ounces cream cheese
1 cup sugar
¼ cup whipping cream
3 tablespoons cornstarch
4 large eggs
¼ cup vanilla extract
¾ teaspoon almond extract
¼ cup vanilla flavored liqueur

In a large bowl, beat cream cheese, sugar, cream, and cornstarch with an electric mixer until smooth. Add eggs one at a time, beating well after each addition. Stir in vanilla and almond extracts and vanilla liqueur. Pour filling onto crust. Bake at 350 degrees for 15 minutes.

REDUCE HEAT TO 200 DEGREES and bake for 2 hours, or until center is firm and no longer looks wet or shiny. Remove cake from oven and carefully run a knife around inside edge of pan. Turn oven off and return cake to it for an additional 2 hours. Chill overnight.

i ♥ cheesecake

warm cherry topping

warm cherry topping

2 17-ounce jars maraschino cherries
1 tablespoon cornstarch

Drain cherries, reserving 1½ cups of liquid (add water if necessary to make a total of 1½ cups). In a small heavy saucepan, stir together reserved cherry liquid and cornstarch. Cook and stir until thickened and bubbly. Cook and stir 2 minutes more. Spread 1 cup of cherry mixture over cheesecake. Set aside remaining cherry mixture. Arrange cherries on top. Chill until serving time.

almond whipped cream

1 cup whipping cream
1 tablespoon powdered sugar
¼ teaspoon almond extract

Just before serving, in a small bowl, beat cream, powdered sugar, and almond extract until it begins to thicken. Reheat remaining cherry mixture in a small saucepan. Pool whipped topping on individual serving plates. Spoon some of the heated cherry mixture over whipped topping. Using a knife, gently swirl mixture to marble it. Place sliced cheesecake on plates.

notes

yogurt

yogurt cheesecakes

Making yogurt cheese from plain yogurt is exciting! Yogurt makes a beautiful, snowy white soft cheese. With the use of a strainer and cheesecloth, natural yogurt loses about 65% of its weight after draining over a 24-hour period. Six pounds of yogurt before draining should yield up to two pounds of cheese—and perhaps a little over with the weight of the cheesecloth included.

When buying yogurt for a cheesecake, it is important to buy a *natural* yogurt, one without gelatin or pectin. If there is gelatin in the yogurt, it will not drain—or, at most, it will drain only a small amount. When reading these recipes, you will notice that after the whey is drained, I add gelatin to the yogurt batter. This is to give the finished product a more stable structure and a firmer consistency. I also beat two whole eggs and four egg whites, along with one envelope of whipped topping mix and some sugar, to give added body and volume to these cakes.

Adding 8 ounces of cream cheese to each yogurt cheesecake adds flavor and texture, and the taste of a "real" cheesecake. Neither my test group nor I were happy until I produced a product that tasted "real." Besides, tasting real gives these cheesecakes an even more impressive presentation.

Another bonus of yogurt cheese is it absorbs flavor from any added ingredient. This offers many options for a variety of cheesecake flavors.

Yogurt cheese is healthier than cream cheese. It has about one-third fewer calories as well as less cholesterol. For 2 pounds of yogurt cheese and 8 ounces of cream cheese—the amounts used in the following recipes—the cholesterol count is 604 mg. Two whole eggs add an additional 548 mg, for a total of 1,152 mg per cheesecake (64 mg per 1½-inch slice). A cheesecake made with 2 pounds of cream cheese and 4 whole eggs has a cholesterol count of 1,992 mg (111 mg per 1½-inch slice), an increase of 73%. Taking another step in the right direction, I cut two egg yolks from each yogurt cheesecake. This further reduces the cholesterol by 548 mg.

There is a "no calorie sweetener" on the market that can be used interchangeably with sugar for baking, supposedly, cup for cup. I tried this and it works! However, the cheesecake doesn't taste quite the same. I find it desirable to add additional "no calorie sweetener" to boost the sweetness. So, for 1 cup of granulated sugar, I use 1⅓ cups of "no calorie sweetener." Another problem I encountered with "no calorie sweetener" is that it absorbs moisture from the cake. If a small taste difference and a somewhat dryer cake do not matter, this is a good way to go, because it does save a lot of calories. I used a "no calorie sweetener" product when creating some of these recipes, and it works best when adjusting each recipe individually. I tried this on my test group, without telling them what I had done. On their comment sheets, each mentioned, "we can tell you have done something different. . . . We like the other recipe better, however, this is fairly good."

Yogurt is a versatile dairy product, and I am glad to have firsthand experience working with it. It has opened many doors for me, and it will for you, too. I am so proud of this chapter in my book. I hope you enjoy the yogurt cheesecakes, for they are worth the small extra effort it takes to make them. They are so delicious that they fool everyone into thinking they are eating old-fashioned cheesecake made with all the traditional ingredients.

For each of the following recipes, you will need to make yogurt cheese.

yogurt cheese

To make 2 pounds of yogurt cheese, drain the whey from 6 pounds of plain yogurt (should not contain any gelatin or pectin). Three 32-ounce containers of yogurt should yield between 2 pounds and 2 pounds 4 ounces of yogurt cheese.

Line a large strainer with cheesecloth and place strainer over a large bowl. Place 3 quarts yogurt inside the cheesecloth and refrigerate overnight to drain. After draining, weigh the yogurt cheese. If the weight is 2 pounds—and no more than 2 pounds 4 ounces—no additional draining is necessary. If the weight is more than 2 pounds 4 ounces, wrap a bath towel around the cheese and cheesecloth to remove additional whey. This may take up to 15 minutes.

AMARETTO YOGURT CHEESECAKE

Make yogurt cheese (p. 235).

chocolate cookie crust

18 chocolate sandwich creme filled cookies, with fillings intact
5 tablespoons butter or margarine, softened

Crush cookies to make crumbs. Place crumbs in a mixing bowl and add butter, mix well. Press crumb mixture evenly onto bottom of greased 9-inch cheesecake pan. Set aside.

Have all ingredients at room temperature. Preheat over to 350 degrees.

amaretto yogurt filling

2 pounds yogurt cheese, after draining from 3 32-ounce containers
8 ounces cream cheese, room temperature
1¼ cups sugar
1 tablespoon cornstarch
2 teaspoons vanilla extract
2 teaspoons almond extract
½ cup Amaretto
2 envelopes unflavored gelatin, dissolved in ⅓ cup boiling water
4 egg whites, from large eggs
2 eggs
1 envelope whipped topping mix
⅓ cup sugar

In a large bowl, combine yogurt cheese and cream cheese, add 1¼ cups sugar and cornstarch using an electric mixer. Beat until smooth and creamy. Stir in vanilla and almond extracts and Amaretto.

i ♥ cheesecake

Stir completely dissolved gelatin into mixture. Set aside. In a large bowl, beat egg whites, whole eggs, and whipped topping mix with an electric mixer until mixture starts to thicken. Slowly add ⅓ cup sugar while beating. Beat until mixture thickens; this should take about 4–5 minutes. Do not double the volume. Stir egg mixture into batter until well blended. Pour batter onto crust. Bake at 350 degrees for 15 minutes.

REDUCE HEAT TO 200 DEGREES and bake for 2 hours, or until center is firm and no longer looks wet or shiny. Remove cake from oven and carefully run a knife around inside edge of pan. Turn oven off and return cake to it for an additional 2 hours. Chill overnight.

whipped topping with marmalade

¼ cup cold milk
1 teaspoon almond extract
1 envelope whipped topping mix
¼ cup orange marmalade
¼ cup almonds, chopped (optional)
chocolate ice cream topping (the type that forms a hardened shell) (optional)

In a small bowl, beat milk, almond extract, and whipped topping mix with an electric mixer until thickened. Fold in marmalade. Spread topping over cake. Garnish by sprinkling with almonds and drizzling chocolate topping over cake. Chill until serving time.

Per 1½-inch slice—Calories: 306 ♥ Fat: 15g ♥ Cholesterol: 64mg ♥ Protein: 8g ♥ Carbohydrates: 35g

BANANA YOGURT CHEESECAKE

Make yogurt cheese (p. 235).

vanilla cookie crust

18 vanilla sandwich creme filled cookies, with fillings intact
5 tablespoons butter or margarine, softened

Crush cookies to make fine crumbs. Place crumbs in a mixing bowl and add butter, mix well. Press crumb mixture evenly onto bottom of greased 9-inch cheesecake pan. Set aside.

Have all ingredients at room temperature. Preheat over to 350 degrees.

banana yogurt filling

2 pounds yogurt cheese, after draining from 3 32-ounce containers
8 ounces cream cheese, room temperature
1 cup sugar
1 tablespoon cornstarch
2 teaspoons vanilla extract
1 tablespoon banana flavoring
1 teaspoon butter flavoring
¾ cup banana, mashed (2 medium bananas)
2 envelopes unflavored gelatin, dissolved in ⅓ cup boiling water
4 egg whites, from large eggs
2 eggs
1 envelope whipped topping mix
⅓ cup sugar

In a large bowl, combine yogurt cheese and cream cheese, add 1 cup sugar and cornstarch using an electric mixer. Beat until smooth and creamy. Stir in vanilla extract and banana and butter flavorings.

i ♥ cheesecake

Stir in mashed bananas. Continue stirring until mixture is well blended. Stir completely dissolved gelatin into mixture. Set aside. In a large bowl, beat egg whites, whole eggs, and whipped topping mix with an electric mixer until mixture starts to thicken. Slowly add ⅓ cup sugar while beating. Beat until mixture thickens; this should take about 4–5 minutes. Do not double the volume. Stir egg mixture into batter until well blended. Pour batter onto crust. Bake at 350 degrees for 15 minutes.

REDUCE HEAT TO 200 DEGREES and bake for 2 hours, or until center is firm and no longer looks wet or shiny. Remove cake from oven and carefully run a knife around inside edge of pan. Turn oven off and return cake to it for an additional 2 hours. Chill overnight.

easy banana topping

¼ cup cold milk
1 teaspoon banana flavoring
1 envelope whipped topping mix
¼ cup banana, mashed (less than half of a medium banana)

In a small bowl, beat milk, banana flavoring, and whipped topping mix with an electric mixer until thickened. Fold mashed banana into topping. Spread topping over cake. Keep chilled.

Per 1½-inch slice—Calories: 296 ♥ Fat: 15g ♥ Cholesterol: 64mg ♥ Protein: 8g ♥ Carbohydrates: 32g

BLUEBERRY YOGURT CHEESECAKE

Make yogurt cheese (p. 235).

lemon cookie crust

18 lemon sandwich creme filled cookies, with fillings intact
5 tablespoons butter or margarine, softened

Crush cookies to make fine crumbs. Place crumbs in a mixing bowl and add butter, mix well. Press crumb mixture evenly onto bottom of greased 9-inch cheesecake pan. Set aside.

Have all ingredients at room temperature. Preheat over to 350 degrees.

blueberry yogurt filling

2 pounds yogurt cheese, after draining from 3 32-ounce containers
8 ounces cream cheese, room temperature
1 cup sugar
1 tablespoon cornstarch
2 teaspoons vanilla extract
1 tablespoon lemon extract
1 teaspoon butter flavoring
⅓ cup blueberry spreadable fruit (found in the jelly section)
1 cup blueberries
2 envelopes unflavored gelatin, dissolved in ⅓ cup boiling water
4 egg whites, from large eggs
2 eggs
1 envelope whipped topping mix
⅓ cup sugar

i ♥ cheesecake

In a large bowl, combine yogurt cheese and cream cheese, add 1 cup sugar and cornstarch using an electric mixer. Beat until smooth and creamy. Stir in vanilla and lemon extracts and butter flavoring. Stir in blueberry spreadable fruit and blueberries, continue stirring until mixture is well blended. Stir completely dissolved gelatin into mixture. Set aside. In a large bowl, beat egg whites, whole eggs, and whipped topping mix with an electric mixer until mixture starts to thicken. Slowly add ⅓ cup sugar while beating. Beat until mixture thickens; this should take about 4–5 minutes. Do not double the volume. Stir egg mixture into batter until well blended. Pour batter onto crust. Bake at 350 degrees for 15 minutes.

REDUCE HEAT TO 200 DEGREES and bake for 2 hours, or until center is firm and no longer looks wet or shiny. Remove cake from oven and carefully run a knife around inside edge of pan. Turn oven off and return cake to it for an additional 2 hours. Chill overnight.

easy blueberry topping

¼ cup cold milk
1 teaspoon lemon extract
1 envelope whipped topping mix
¼ cup blueberry spreadable fruit
¼ cup blueberries

In a small bowl, beat milk, lemon extract, and whipped topping mix with an electric mixer until thickened. Fold blueberry spreadable fruit and blueberries into topping. Spread topping over cake. Keep chilled.

Per 1½-inch slice — Calories: 302 ♥ Fat: 15g ♥ Cholesterol: 64mg ♥ Protein: 8g ♥ Carbohydrates: 34g

CARAMEL CREME YOGURT CHEESECAKE

Make yogurt cheese (p. 235).

vanilla cookie crust

18 vanilla sandwich creme filled cookies, with fillings intact
5 tablespoons butter or margarine, softened

Crush cookies to make fine crumbs. Place crumbs in a mixing bowl and add butter, mix well. Press crumb mixture evenly onto bottom of greased 9-inch cheesecake pan. Set aside.

Have all ingredients at room temperature. Preheat over to 350 degrees.

caramel yogurt filling

2 pounds yogurt cheese, after draining from 3 32-ounce containers
8 ounces cream cheese, room temperature
1½ cups dark brown sugar
1 tablespoon cornstarch
1 cup caramel sauce (found in grocer's ice cream section)
1 tablespoon vanilla extract
2 teaspoons butter flavoring
2 envelopes unflavored gelatin, dissolved in ⅓ cup boiling water
4 egg whites, from large eggs
2 eggs
1 envelope whipped topping mix
⅓ cup sugar

In a large bowl, combine yogurt cheese, cream cheese, brown sugar, cornstarch, and caramel sauce with an electric mixer until smooth. Stir in vanilla extract and butter flavoring. Stir completely

i ♥ cheesecake

dissolved gelatin into mixture. Set aside. In a large bowl, beat egg whites, whole eggs, and whipped topping mix with an electric mixer until mixture starts to thicken. Slowly add sugar while beating. Beat until mixture thickens; this should take about 4–5 minutes. Do not double the volume. Stir egg mixture into batter until well blended. Pour batter onto crust. Bake at 350 degrees for 15 minutes.

REDUCE HEAT TO 200 DEGREES and bake for 2 hours, or until center is firm and no longer looks wet or shiny. Remove cake from oven and carefully run a knife around inside edge of pan. Turn oven off and return cake to it for an additional 2 hours. Chill overnight.

white chocolate topping

4 ounces white chocolate chips
3 tablespoons sour cream
1 tablespoon caramel sauce
caramel ice cream topping(the type that forms a hardened shell) (optional)
¼ cup pecans (optional)

In a small heavy saucepan, melt white chocolate, sour cream, and caramel sauce over low heat, stirring constantly. After melting, spread over cheesecake. Garnish by drizzling caramel topping over cake. Sprinkle with pecans, if desired. Keep chilled.

Per 1½-inch slice — Calories: 375 ♥ Fat: 13g ♥ Cholesterol: 65mg ♥ Protein: 8g ♥ Carbohydrates: 47g

CARROT ORANGE YOGURT CHEESECAKE

Make yogurt cheese (p. 235).

vanilla cookie crust

18 vanilla sandwich creme filled cookies, with fillings intact
5 tablespoons butter or margarine, softened

Crush cookies to make fine crumbs. Place crumbs in a mixing bowl and add butter, mix well. Press crumb mixture evenly onto bottom of greased 9-inch cheesecake pan. Set aside.

Have all ingredients at room temperature. Preheat over to 350 degrees.

carrot orange yogurt filling

2 pounds yogurt cheese, after draining from 3 32-ounce containers
8 ounces cream cheese, room temperature
1½ cups sugar
1 tablespoon cornstarch
2 teaspoons cinnamon
2 teaspoons vanilla extract
1 tablespoon orange extract
4 ounces frozen concentrated orange juice, thawed
2 envelopes unflavored gelatin, dissolved in ⅓ cup boiling water
2 medium sized carrots, grated
4 egg whites, from large eggs
2 eggs
1 envelope whipped topping mix
⅓ cup sugar

i ♥ cheesecake

In a large bowl, combine yogurt cheese and cream cheese, add 1½ cups sugar, cornstarch, and cinnamon using an electric mixer. Beat until smooth and creamy. Stir in vanilla and orange extracts and orange juice. Stir completely dissolved gelatin into mixture. Stir in carrots. Set aside. In a large bowl, beat egg whites, whole eggs, and whipped topping mix with an electric mixer until mixture starts to thicken. Slowly add ⅓ cup sugar while beating. Beat until mixture thickens; this should take about 4–5 minutes. Do not double the volume. Stir egg mixture into batter until well blended. Pour batter onto crust. Bake at 350 degrees for 15 minutes.

REDUCE HEAT TO 200 DEGREES and bake for 2 hours, or until center is firm and no longer looks wet or shiny. Remove cake from oven and carefully run a knife around inside edge of pan. Turn oven off and return cake to it for an additional 2 hours. Chill overnight.

white chocolate orange topping

4 ounces white chocolate, melted
¼ cup sour cream
1 teaspoon orange extract
chocolate ice cream topping (the type that forms a hardened shell) (optional)
¼ cup pecans, chopped (optional)

In a small heavy saucepan, melt chocolate and sour cream over low heat, stirring constantly until melted and smooth. Stir in orange extract. Spread topping over cake. Drizzle chocolate ice cream topping over cake, creating a design. Sprinkle with pecans, if desired. Keep chilled.

Per 1½-inch slice—Calories: 343 ♥ Fat: 17g ♥ Cholesterol: 65mg ♥ Protein: 8g ♥ Carbohydrates: 40g

CHOCOLATE CARAMEL YOGURT CHEESECAKE

Make yogurt cheese (p. 235).

chocolate cookie crust

18 chocolate sandwich creme filled cookies, with fillings intact
5 tablespoons butter or margarine, softened

Crush cookies to make fine crumbs. Place crumbs in a mixing bowl and add butter, mix well. Press crumb mixture evenly onto bottom of greased 9-inch cheesecake pan. Set aside.

Have all ingredients at room temperature. Preheat over to 350 degrees.

chocolate caramel yogurt filling

2 pounds yogurt cheese, after draining from 3 32-ounce containers
8 ounces cream cheese, room temperature
¾ cup dark brown sugar
¾ cup granulated sugar
1 tablespoon cornstarch
⅓ cup dark corn syrup
2 teaspoons vanilla extract
2 teaspoons butter flavoring
12 ounces milk chocolate chips, melted
2 envelopes unflavored gelatin, dissolved in ⅓ cup boiling water
4 egg whites, from large eggs
2 eggs
1 envelope whipped topping mix
⅓ cup sugar

i ♥ cheesecake

In a large bowl, combine yogurt cheese, cream cheese, brown sugar, ¾ cup sugar, cornstarch, and corn syrup with an electric mixer until smooth. Stir in vanilla extract and butter flavoring. Completely stir in melted chocolate and gelatin. Set aside. In a large bowl, beat egg whites, whole eggs, and whipped topping mix with an electric mixer until mixture starts to thicken. Slowly add ⅓ cup sugar while beating. Beat until mixture thickens; this should take about 4–5 minutes. Do not double the volume. Stir egg mixture into batter until well blended. Pour batter onto crust. Bake at 350 degrees for 15 minutes.

REDUCE HEAT TO 200 DEGREES and bake for 2 hours, or until center is firm and no longer looks wet or shiny. Remove cake from oven and carefully run a knife around inside edge of pan. Turn oven off and return cake to it for an additional 2 hours. Chill overnight.

chocolate topping

5 ounces milk chocolate chips
¼ cup sour cream

In a small heavy saucepan, melt chocolate chips and sour cream over low heat, stirring constantly. After melting, spread over cheesecake. Keep chilled.

Per 1½-inch slice—Calories: 452 ♥ Fat: 15g ♥ Cholesterol: 65mg ♥ Protein: 9g ♥ Carbohydrates: 52g

CHOCOLATE MINT YOGURT CHEESECAKE

Make yogurt cheese (p. 235).

chocolate cookie crust

18 chocolate sandwich creme filled cookies, with fillings intact
5 tablespoons butter or margarine, softened

Crush cookies to make fine crumbs. Place crumbs in a mixing bowl and add butter, mix well. Press crumb mixture evenly onto bottom of greased 9-inch cheesecake pan. Set aside.

Have all ingredients at room temperature. Preheat over to 350 degrees.

chocolate mint yogurt filling

2 pounds yogurt cheese, after draining from 3 32-ounce containers
8 ounces cream cheese, room temperature
1½ cups sugar
1 tablespoon cornstarch
2 teaspoons vanilla extract
1 tablespoon mint flavoring
12 ounces semisweet chocolate chips, melted
2 envelopes unflavored gelatin, dissolved in ⅓ cup boiling water
4 egg whites, from large eggs
2 eggs
1 envelope whipped topping mix
⅓ cup sugar

In a large bowl, combine yogurt cheese, cream cheese, 1½ cups sugar, and cornstarch with an electric mixer until smooth. Stir in vanilla and mint extracts. Thoroughly stir in melted chocolate and gelatin.

i ♥ cheesecake

Set aside. In a large bowl, beat egg whites, whole eggs, and whipped topping mix with an electric mixer until mixture starts to thicken. Slowly add ⅓ cup sugar while beating. Beat until mixture thickens; this should take about 4–5 minutes. Do not double the volume. Stir egg mixture into batter until well blended. Pour batter onto crust. Bake at 350 degrees for 15 minutes.

REDUCE HEAT TO 200 DEGREES and bake for 2 hours, or until center is firm and no longer looks wet or shiny. Remove cake from oven and carefully run a knife around inside edge of pan. Turn oven off and return cake to it for an additional 2 hours. Chill overnight.

crème de menthe topping

¼ cup green crème de menthe, very cold
¼ cup milk, very cold
2 envelopes whipped topping mix
chocolate ice cream topping (the type that forms a hardened shell) (optional)

In a medium bowl, beat cold crème de menthe, milk, and whipped topping mix with an electric mixer until thickened. Spread over cake. Drizzle chocolate over top. Keep chilled.

Per 1½-inch slice—Calories: 415 ♥ Fat: 20g ♥ Cholesterol: 64mg ♥ Protein: 10g ♥ Carbohydrates: 47g

CHOCOLATE PEANUT BUTTER
YOGURT CHEESECAKE

Make yogurt cheese (p. 235).

peanut butter cookie crust

18 peanut butter sandwich creme filled cookies, with fillings intact
5 tablespoons butter or margarine, softened

Crush cookies to make crumbs. Place crumbs in a mixing bowl and add butter, mix well. Press crumb mixture evenly onto bottom of greased 9-inch cheesecake pan. Set aside.

Have all ingredients at room temperature. Preheat over to 350 degrees.

chocolate peanut butter yogurt filling

2 pounds yogurt cheese, after draining from 3 32-ounce containers
8 ounces cream cheese, room temperature
1¼ cups dark brown sugar
1 tablespoon cornstarch
1 tablespoon vanilla extract
1 cup creamy peanut butter
12 ounces semisweet chocolate chips, melted
2 envelopes unflavored gelatin, dissolved in ⅓ cup boiling water
4 egg whites, from large eggs
2 eggs
1 envelope whipped topping mix
⅓ cup sugar

In a large bowl, combine yogurt cheese and cream cheese, add brown sugar and cornstarch using an electric mixer. Beat until smooth and creamy. Stir in vanilla extract and peanut butter. Thoroughly stir in melted chocolate chips and gelatin. Set aside. In a large bowl, beat egg whites, whole eggs, and whipped topping mix with an electric mixer until mixture starts to thicken. Slowly add sugar while beating. Beat until mixture thickens; this should take about 4–5 minutes. Do not double the volume. Stir the egg mixture into the chocolate batter until well blended. Pour batter onto crust. Bake at 350 degrees for 15 minutes.

REDUCE HEAT TO 200 DEGREES and bake for 2 hours, or until center is firm and no longer looks wet or shiny. Remove cake from oven and carefully run a knife around inside edge of pan. Turn oven off and return cake to it for an additional 2 hours. Chill overnight.

peanut butter topping

4 ounces peanut butter chips
¼ cup sour cream
chocolate ice cream topping (the type that forms a hardened shell) (optional)
peanuts, for garnish

In a small heavy saucepan, melt peanut butter chips and sour cream over low heat, stirring constantly until melted and smooth. Spread topping over cake. Garnish with chocolate topping by drizzling it over the top, and sprinkle with peanuts. Keep chilled.

Per 1½-inch slice — Calories: 501 ♥ Fat: 29g ♥ Cholesterol: 65mg ♥ Protein: 15g ♥ Carbohydrates: 47g

COFFEE CREME CARAMEL
YOGURT CHEESECAKE

Make yogurt cheese (p. 235).

vanilla cookie crust

18 vanilla sandwich creme filled cookies, with filling intact

2 teaspoons instant coffee, dissolved in 2 teaspoons boiling water

5 tablespoons butter or margarine, softened

Crush cookies to make fine crumbs. Place crumbs and dissolved coffee in a mixing bowl and add butter, mix well. Press crumb mixture evenly onto bottom of greased 9-inch cheesecake pan. Set aside.

Have all ingredients at room temperature. Preheat over to 350 degrees.

caramel coffee yogurt filling

2 pounds yogurt cheese, after draining from 3 32-ounce containers

8 ounces cream cheese, room temperature

½ cup sugar

½ cup brown sugar

1 tablespoon cornstarch

1 tablespoon vanilla extract

1 tablespoon butter flavoring

½ cup "Creme Caramel" (a naturally and artificially flavored coffee drink mix—this is one of the International Coffees)

½ cup 2% milk, hot, not boiling

2 envelopes unflavored gelatin, dissolved in ⅓ cup boiling water

4 egg whites, from large eggs

2 eggs

1 envelope whipped topping mix

⅓ cup sugar

i ♥ cheesecake

In a large bowl, combine yogurt cheese and cream cheese, add ½ cup sugar, brown sugar, and corn-starch using an electric mixer. Beat until smooth and creamy. Stir in vanilla extract and butter fla-voring. Combine coffee and milk and stir into batter. Stir completely dissolved gelatin into mixture. Set aside. In a large bowl, beat egg whites, whole eggs, and whipped topping mix with an electric mixer until mixture starts to thicken. Slowly add ⅓ cup sugar while beating. Beat until mixture thick-ens; this should take about 4–5 minutes. Do not double the volume. Stir egg mixture into batter un-til well blended. Pour batter onto crust. Bake at 350 degrees for 15 minutes.

REDUCE HEAT TO 200 DEGREES and bake for 2 hours, or until center is firm and no longer looks wet or shiny. Remove cake from oven and carefully run a knife around inside edge of pan. Turn oven off and return cake to it for an additional 2 hours. Chill overnight.

mocha topping

4 ounces white chocolate
¼ cup sour cream
1 teaspoon instant coffee, dissolved in 2 teaspoons boiling water
caramel ice cream topping (the type that forms a hardened shell) (optional)

In a small heavy saucepan, melt chocolate and sour cream over low heat, stirring constantly until melted and smooth. Stir in dissolved coffee. Spread topping over cake. Drizzle ice cream topping over top. Keep chilled.

Per 1½-inch slice—Calories: 301 ♥ Fat: 16g ♥ Cholesterol: 66mg ♥ Protein: 8g ♥ Carbohydrates: 30g

CREAMY PEANUT BUTTER
YOGURT CHEESECAKE

Make yogurt cheese (p. 235).

chocolate wafer crust

8 ounces chocolate wafers

5 tablespoons butter or margarine, softened

Crush cookies to make crumbs. Place crumbs in a mixing bowl and add butter, mix well. Press crumb mixture evenly onto bottom of greased 9-inch cheesecake pan. Set aside.

Have all ingredients at room temperature. Preheat over to 350 degrees.

peanut butter yogurt filling

2 pounds yogurt cheese, after draining from 3 32-ounce containers

8 ounces cream cheese, room temperature

1½ cups dark brown sugar

1 tablespoon cornstarch

2 teaspoons vanilla extract

1 cup creamy peanut butter

2 envelopes unflavored gelatin, dissolved in ⅓ cup boiling water

4 egg whites, from large eggs

2 eggs

1 envelope whipped topping mix

⅓ cup sugar

In a large bowl, combine yogurt cheese and cream cheese, add brown sugar and cornstarch using an electric mixer. Beat until smooth and creamy. Thoroughly stir in vanilla extract and peanut butter.

Stir completely dissolved gelatin into mixture. Set aside. In a large bowl, beat egg whites, whole eggs, and whipped topping mix with an electric mixer until mixture starts to thicken. Slowly add sugar while beating. Beat until mixture thickens; this should take about 4–5 minutes. Do not double the volume. Stir egg mixture into chocolate batter until well blended. Pour batter onto crust. Bake at 350 degrees for 15 minutes.

REDUCE HEAT TO 200 DEGREES and bake for 2 hours, or until center is firm and no longer looks wet or shiny. Remove cake from oven and carefully run a knife around inside edge of pan. Turn oven off and return cake to it for an additional 2 hours. Chill overnight.

chocolate caramel topping

4 ounces milk chocolate chips
2 tablespoons sour cream
2 tablespoons creamy peanut butter
peanuts

In a small heavy saucepan, melt chocolate chips, sour cream, and peanut butter over low heat, stirring constantly until melted and smooth. Spread topping over cake. Garnish top of cake with peanuts. Keep chilled.

Per 1½-inch slice—Calories: 448 ♥ Fat: 25g ♥ Cholesterol: 65mg ♥ Protein: 13g ♥ Carbohydrates: 38g

GERMAN CHOCOLATE YOGURT CHEESECAKE

Make yogurt cheese (p. 235).

coconut cookie crust

18 coconut cookies

5 tablespoons butter or margarine, softened

Crush cookies to make fine crumbs. Place crumbs in a mixing bowl and add butter, mix well. Press crumb mixture evenly onto bottom of greased 9-inch cheesecake pan. Set aside.

Have all ingredients at room temperature. Preheat over to 350 degrees.

german chocolate yogurt filling

2 pounds yogurt cheese, after draining from 3 32-ounce containers

8 ounces cream cheese, room temperature

¾ cup dark brown sugar

¾ cup granulated sugar

1 tablespoon cornstarch

1 tablespoon vanilla extract

2 teaspoons butter flavoring

12 ounces German chocolate, melted

2 envelopes unflavored gelatin, dissolved in ⅓ cup boiling water

4 egg whites, from large eggs

2 eggs

1 envelope whipped topping mix

⅓ cup sugar

In a large bowl, combine yogurt cheese, cream cheese, brown sugar, ¾ cup sugar, and cornstarch with an electric mixer until smooth. Stir in vanilla extract and butter flavoring. Completely stir in melted chocolate and gelatin. Set aside. In a large bowl, beat egg whites, whole eggs, and whipped topping mix with an electric mixer until mixture starts to thicken. Slowly add ⅓ cup sugar while beating. Beat until mixture thickens; this should take about 4–5 minutes. Do not double the volume. Stir egg mixture into batter until well blended. Pour batter onto crust. Bake at 350 degrees for 15 minutes.

REDUCE HEAT TO 200 DEGREES and bake for 2 hours, or until center is firm and no longer looks wet or shiny. Remove cake from oven and carefully run a knife around inside edge of pan. Turn oven off and return cake to it for an additional 2 hours. Chill overnight.

coconut pecan topping

4 tablespoons butter or margarine
⅓ cup sugar
⅓ cup evaporated milk
1 egg yolk, lightly beaten
1 cup coconut, grated (reserve ⅓ cup for decoration)
⅔ cup pecans, chopped
2 teaspoons vanilla extract
whole pecans
chocolate ice cream topping (the type that forms a hardened shell) (optional)

In a small heavy saucepan, melt butter. Stir in sugar, evaporated milk, and egg yolk. Cook over low heat, stirring constantly until thickened. Stir in coconut, pecans, and vanilla extract. Spread over cake. Decorate with reserved coconut and pecans. Drizzle chocolate over top, creating a design. Keep chilled.

Per 1½-inch slice — Calories: 467 ♥ Fat: 21g ♥ Cholesterol: 83mg ♥ Protein: 8g ♥ Carbohydrates: 50g

IRISH MOCHA YOGURT CHEESECAKE

Make yogurt cheese (p. 235).

mocha cookie crust

18 chocolate sandwich creme filled cookies, with fillings intact
2 teaspoons instant coffee, dissolved in 2 teaspoons boiling water
5 tablespoons butter or margarine, softened

Crush cookies to make fine crumbs. Place crumbs and dissolved coffee in a mixing bowl and add butter, mix well. Press crumb mixture evenly onto bottom of greased 9-inch cheesecake pan. Set aside.

Have all ingredients at room temperature. Preheat over to 350 degrees.

mocha yogurt filling

2 pounds yogurt cheese, after draining from 3 32-ounce containers
8 ounces cream cheese, room temperature
1½ cups sugar
1 tablespoon cornstarch
¼ cup cocoa
2 teaspoons vanilla extract
2 teaspoons instant coffee, dissolved in 2 teaspoons boiling water
6 ounces milk chocolate chips, melted
½ cup Irish Creme liqueur
2 envelopes unflavored gelatin, dissolved in ⅓ cup boiling water
4 egg whites, from large eggs
2 eggs
1 envelope whipped topping mix
⅓ cup sugar

i ♥ cheesecake

In a large bowl, beat yogurt cheese, cream cheese, 1½ cups sugar, cornstarch, and cocoa with an electric mixer until smooth. Stir in vanilla extract and instant coffee. Stir in melted chocolate. Stir in Irish Creme liqueur and dissolved gelatin. Set aside. In a large bowl, beat egg whites, whole eggs, and whipped topping mix with an electric mixer until mixture starts to thicken. Slowly add ⅓ cup sugar while beating. Beat until mixture thickens; this should take about 4–5 minutes. Do not double the volume. Stir egg mixture into batter until well blended. Pour batter onto crust. Bake at 350 degrees for 15 minutes.

REDUCE HEAT TO 200 DEGREES and bake for 2 hours, or until center is firm and no longer looks wet or shiny. Remove cake from oven and carefully run a knife around inside edge of pan. Turn oven off and return cake to it for an additional 2 hours. Chill overnight.

mocha whipped topping

⅓ cup milk, very cold
2 envelopes whipped topping mix
2 tablespoons powdered sugar
1 tablespoon cocoa
1 teaspoon instant coffee, dissolved in 1 teaspoon boiling water
chocolate ice cream topping (the type that forms a hardened shell) (optional)

In a medium bowl, beat cold milk, whipped topping mix, powdered sugar, cocoa, and dissolved instant coffee with an electric mixer until thickened. Spread over cake. Drizzle chocolate over top. Keep chilled.

Per 1½-inch slice—Calories: 370 ♥ Fat: 15g ♥ Cholesterol: 64mg ♥ Protein: 9g ♥ Carbohydrates: 42g

KEY LIME YOGURT CHEESECAKE

Make yogurt cheese (p. 235).

vanilla cookie crust

18 vanilla sandwich creme filled cookies, with filling intact
5 tablespoons butter or margarine, softened

Crush cookies to make crumbs. Place crumbs in a mixing bowl and add butter, mix well. Press crumb mixture evenly onto bottom of greased 9-inch cheesecake pan. Set aside.

Have all ingredients at room temperature. Preheat over to 350 degrees.

key lime yogurt filling

2 pounds yogurt cheese, after draining from 3 32-ounce containers
8 ounces cream cheese, room temperature
14 ounces sweetened condensed milk
1 cup sugar
1 tablespoon cornstarch
2 teaspoons vanilla extract
⅔ cup key lime juice
1 teaspoon lime zest
2 envelopes unflavored gelatin, dissolved in ⅓ cup boiling water
4 egg whites, from large eggs
2 eggs
1 envelope whipped topping mix
⅓ cup sugar

In a large bowl, combine yogurt cheese and cream cheese, add sweetened condensed milk, 1 cup sugar, and cornstarch using an electric mixer. Beat until smooth and creamy. Stir in vanilla extract, key lime juice, and lime zest. Stir completely dissolved gelatin into mixture. Set aside. In a large bowl, beat egg whites, whole eggs, and whipped topping mix with an electric mixer until mixture starts to thicken. Slowly add ⅓ cup sugar while beating. Beat until mixture thickens; this should take about 4–5 minutes. Do not double the volume. Stir egg mixture into batter until well blended. Pour batter onto crust. Bake at 350 degrees for 15 minutes.

REDUCE HEAT TO 200 DEGREES and bake for 2 hours, or until center is firm and no longer looks wet or shiny. Remove cake from oven and carefully run a knife around inside edge of pan. Turn oven off and return cake to it for an additional 2 hours. Chill overnight.

orange marmalade whipped topping

¼ cup cold milk
1 envelope whipped topping mix
2 tablespoons orange marmalade

In a small bowl, beat milk and whipped topping mix with a mixer on high speed until thickened. Fold in marmalade. Spread topping over cake. Keep chilled.

Per 1½-inch slice—Calories: 362 ♥ Fat: 16g ♥ Cholesterol: 70mg ♥ Protein: 9g ♥ Carbohydrates: 43g

LEMON YOGURT CHEESECAKE

Make yogurt cheese (p. 235).

lemon cookie crust

18 lemon sandwich creme filled cookies, with filling intact
5 tablespoons butter or margarine, softened

Crush cookies to make crumbs. Place crumbs in a mixing bowl and add butter, mix well. Press crumb mixture evenly onto bottom of greased 9-inch cheesecake pan. Set aside.

Have all ingredients at room temperature. Preheat over to 350 degrees.

lemon yogurt filling

2 pounds yogurt cheese, after draining from 3 32-ounce containers
8 ounces cream cheese, room temperature
1 cup sugar
1 tablespoon cornstarch
1 tablespoon lemon extract
1 teaspoon lemon peel, finely grated
6 ounces frozen concentrated lemonade, thawed
2 envelopes unflavored gelatin, dissolved in ⅓ cup boiling water
4 egg whites, from large eggs
2 eggs
1 envelope whipped topping mix
⅓ cup sugar

In a large bowl, combine yogurt cheese and cream cheese, add 1 cup sugar and cornstarch using an electric mixer. Beat until smooth and creamy. Stir in lemon extract, lemon peel, and lemonade and

i ♥ cheesecake

continue stirring until smooth. Stir completely dissolved gelatin into mixture. Set aside. In a large bowl, beat egg whites, whole eggs, and whipped topping mix with an electric mixer until mixture starts to thicken. Slowly add ⅓ cup sugar while beating. Beat until mixture thickens; this should take about 4–5 minutes. Do not double the volume. Stir egg mixture into batter until well blended. Pour batter onto crust. Bake at 350 degrees for 15 minutes.

REDUCE HEAT TO 200 DEGREES and bake for 2 hours, or until center is firm and no longer looks wet or shiny. Remove cake from oven and carefully run a knife around inside edge of pan. Turn oven off and return cake to it for an additional 2 hours. Chill overnight.

white chocolate lemon topping

4 ounces white chocolate
¼ cup sour cream
1½ teaspoons lemon extract
1 drop yellow food coloring

In a small heavy saucepan, melt chocolate and sour cream over low heat, stirring constantly until melted and smooth. Add lemon extract and food coloring. Spread over top of cake. Keep chilled.

Per 1½-inch slice — Calories: 335 ♥ Fat: 17g ♥ Cholesterol: 65mg ♥ Protein: 8g ♥ Carbohydrates: 40g

LIME YOGURT CHEESECAKE

Make yogurt cheese (p. 235).

lemon cookie crust
18 lemon sandwich creme filled cookies, with filling intact
5 tablespoons butter or margarine, softened

Crush cookies to make crumbs. Place crumbs in a mixing bowl and add butter, mix well. Press crumb mixture evenly onto bottom of greased 9-inch cheesecake pan. Set aside.

Have all ingredients at room temperature. Preheat over to 350 degrees.

limeade yogurt filling
2 pounds yogurt cheese, after draining from 3 32-ounce containers
8 ounces cream cheese, room temperature
1 cup sugar
1 tablespoon cornstarch
1 tablespoon fresh lime juice
1 teaspoon lime peel, finely grated
6 ounces frozen concentrated limeade, thawed
2 envelopes unflavored gelatin, dissolved in ⅓ cup boiling water
4 egg whites, from large eggs
2 eggs
1 envelope whipped topping mix
⅓ cup sugar

In a large bowl, combine yogurt cheese and cream cheese, add 1 cup sugar and cornstarch using an electric mixer. Beat until smooth and creamy. Stir in lime juice, lime peel, and limeade and continue

i ♥ cheesecake

stirring until smooth. Stir completely dissolved gelatin into mixture. Set aside. In a large bowl, beat egg whites, whole eggs, and whipped topping mix with an electric mixer until mixture starts to thicken. Slowly add ⅓ cup sugar while beating. Beat until mixture thickens; this should take about 4–5 minutes. Do not double the volume. Stir egg mixture into batter until well blended. Pour batter onto crust. Bake at 350 degrees for 15 minutes.

REDUCE HEAT TO 200 DEGREES and bake for 2 hours, or until center is firm and no longer looks wet or shiny. Remove cake from oven and carefully run a knife around inside edge of pan. Turn oven off and return cake to it for an additional 2 hours. Chill overnight.

white chocolate lime topping

4 ounces white chocolate
¼ cup sour cream
2 teaspoons lime juice
1 drop green food coloring

In a small heavy saucepan, melt chocolate and sour cream over low heat, stirring constantly until melted and smooth. Stir in lime juice and food coloring. Spread topping over cake. Keep chilled.

Per 1½-inch slice—Calories: 333 ♥ Fat: 17g ♥ Cholesterol: 65mg ♥ Protein: 8g ♥ Carbohydrates: 40g

MANDARIN ORANGE WITH
TRIPLE SEC YOGURT CHEESECAKE

Make yogurt cheese (p. 235).

lemon cookie crust

18 lemon sandwich creme filled cookies, with fillings intact
5 tablespoons butter or margarine, softened

Crush cookies to make fine crumbs. Place crumbs in a mixing bowl and add butter, mix well. Press crumb mixture evenly onto bottom of greased 9-inch cheesecake pan. Set aside.

Have all ingredients at room temperature. Preheat over to 350 degrees.

orange liqueur yogurt filling

2 pounds yogurt cheese, after draining from 3 32-ounce containers
8 ounces cream cheese, room temperature
1½ cups sugar
1 tablespoon cornstarch
1 teaspoon grated orange peel
2 teaspoons vanilla extract
1 tablespoon orange extract
1 teaspoon lemon extract
⅓ cup triple sec, or other orange flavored liqueur
2 envelopes unflavored gelatin, dissolved in ⅓ cup boiling water
4 egg whites, from large eggs
2 eggs
1 envelope whipped topping mix
⅓ cup sugar

i ♥ cheesecake

In a large bowl, combine yogurt cheese and cream cheese, add 1½ cups sugar, cornstarch, and orange peel using an electric mixer. Beat until smooth and creamy. Stir in vanilla, orange, and lemon extracts and triple sec. Stir completely dissolved gelatin into mixture. Set aside. In a large bowl, beat egg whites, whole eggs, and whipped topping mix with an electric mixer until mixture starts to thicken. Slowly add ⅓ cup sugar while beating. Beat until mixture thickens; this should take about 4–5 minutes. Do not double the volume. Stir egg mixture into batter until well blended. Pour batter onto crust. Bake at 350 degrees for 15 minutes.

REDUCE HEAT TO 200 DEGREES and bake for 2 hours, or until center is firm and no longer looks wet or shiny. Remove cake from oven and carefully run a knife around inside edge of pan. Turn oven off and return cake to it for an additional 2 hours. Chill overnight.

orange whipped topping

¼ cup milk, very cold
1 envelope whipped topping mix
1 teaspoon orange extract
mandarin orange segments and other fresh fruit in season, sliced

In a small bowl, beat milk, whipped topping mix, and orange extract with an electric mixer until thickened. Spread topping over cake. Garnish with fruit. Keep chilled.

Per 1½-inch slice—Calories: 305 ♥ Fat: 15g ♥ Cholesterol: 64mg ♥ Protein: 8g ♥ Carbohydrates: 33g

MOOSE TRACKS YOGURT CHEESECAKE

Make yogurt cheese (p. 235).

vanilla wafer crust

8 ounces vanilla wafers

5 tablespoons butter or margarine, softened

Crush cookies to make fine crumbs. Place crumbs in a mixing bowl and add butter, mix well. Press crumb mixture evenly onto bottom of greased 9-inch cheesecake pan. Set aside.

Have all ingredients at room temperature. Preheat over to 350 degrees.

peanut butter balls and chocolate yogurt filling

2 pounds yogurt cheese, after draining from 3 32-ounce containers

8 ounces cream cheese, room temperature

1½ cups sugar

1 tablespoon cornstarch

¼ cup vanilla extract, or vanilla flavored liqueur

2 envelopes unflavored gelatin, dissolved in ⅓ cup boiling water

1 cup creamy peanut butter

¾ cup powdered sugar

4 egg whites, from large eggs

2 eggs

1 envelope whipped topping mix

⅓ cup sugar

8 ounce jar of chocolate fudge ice cream topping

In a large bowl, combine yogurt cheese and cream cheese, add 1½ cups sugar and cornstarch using an electric mixer. Beat until smooth and creamy. Stir in vanilla extract. Stir completely dissolved

i ♥ cheesecake

gelatin into mixture. Set aside. In a small bowl, combine peanut butter and powdered sugar. Make nickel-size balls with the mixture and place on a plate. Set aside. In a large bowl, beat egg whites, whole eggs, and whipped topping mix with an electric mixer until mixture starts to thicken. Slowly add ⅓ cup sugar while beating. Beat until mixture thickens; this should take about 4–5 minutes. Do not double the volume. Stir egg mixture into batter until well blended. Pour about ⅓ of batter onto crust. Place ⅓ of small balls on top of batter. Ribbon ⅓ of chocolate topping over balls. Repeat with the next two layers. Bake at 350 degrees for 15 minutes.

REDUCE HEAT TO 200 DEGREES and bake for 2 hours, or until center is firm and no longer looks wet or shiny. Remove cake from oven and carefully run a knife around inside edge of pan. Turn oven off and return cake to it for an additional 2 hours. Chill overnight.

peanut butter topping

¼ cup milk, very cold
1 envelope whipped topping mix
¼ cup creamy peanut butter
chocolate ice cream topping (the type that forms a hardened shell) (optional)
peanuts (optional)

In a small bowl, beat milk and whipped topping mix with an electric mixer until thickened. Fold in peanut butter. Spread topping over cake. Drizzle chocolate ice cream topping over cake. Garnish with peanuts. Keep chilled.

Per 1½-inch slice—Calories: 454 ♥ Fat: 24g ♥ Cholesterol: 64mg ♥ Protein: 12g ♥ Carbohydrates: 55g

ORANGE YOGURT CAPPUCCINO CHEESECAKE

Make yogurt cheese (p. 235).

mocha cookie crust

18 chocolate sandwich creme filled cookies, with filling intact
2 teaspoons instant coffee, dissolved in 2 teaspoons boiling water
5 tablespoons butter or margarine, softened

Crush cookies to make fine crumbs. Place crumbs and dissolved coffee in a mixing bowl and add butter, mix well. Press crumb mixture evenly onto bottom of greased 9-inch cheesecake pan. Set aside.

Have all ingredients at room temperature. Preheat over to 350 degrees.

orange yogurt cappuccino filling

2 pounds yogurt cheese, after draining from 3 32-ounce containers
8 ounces cream cheese, room temperature
1 cup sugar
1 tablespoon cornstarch
2 teaspoons vanilla extract
1 tablespoon orange extract
½ cup "Orange Cappuccino" (a naturally and artificially flavored coffee drink mix—this is one of the International Coffees)
½ cup 2% milk, hot, not boiling
2 envelopes unflavored gelatin, dissolved in ⅓ cup boiling water
4 egg whites, from large eggs
2 eggs
1 envelope whipped topping mix
⅓ cup sugar

i ♥ cheesecake

In a large bowl, combine yogurt cheese and cream cheese, add 1 cup sugar and cornstarch using an electric mixer. Beat until smooth and creamy. Stir in vanilla and orange extracts. Combine coffee and milk and stir into batter. Stir completely dissolved gelatin into mixture. Set aside. In a large bowl, beat egg whites, whole eggs, and whipped topping mix with an electric mixer until mixture starts to thicken. Slowly add ⅓ cup sugar while beating. Beat until mixture thickens; this should take about 4–5 minutes. Do not double the volume. Stir egg mixture into batter until well blended. Pour batter onto crust. Bake at 350 degrees for 15 minutes.

REDUCE HEAT TO 200 DEGREES and bake for 2 hours, or until center is firm and no longer looks wet or shiny. Remove cake from oven and carefully run a knife around inside edge of pan. Turn oven off and return cake to it for an additional 2 hours. Chill overnight.

white chocolate coffee topping

4 ounces white chocolate, melted
¼ cup sour cream
1 teaspoon instant coffee, dissolved in 2 teaspoons boiling water

In a small heavy saucepan, melt chocolate and sour cream over low heat, stirring constantly until melted and smooth. Stir in dissolved coffee. Spread topping over cake. Keep chilled.

Per 1½-inch slice—Calories: 337 ♥ Fat: 18g ♥ Cholesterol: 66mg ♥ Protein: 8g ♥ Carbohydrates: 35g

PEACH YOGURT PECAN CHEESECAKE

Make yogurt cheese (p. 235).

vanilla cookie crust

18 vanilla sandwich creme filled cookies, with fillings intact
5 tablespoons butter or margarine, softened

Crush cookies to make fine crumbs. Place crumbs in a mixing bowl and add butter, mix well. Press crumb mixture evenly onto bottom of greased 9-inch cheesecake pan. Set aside.

Have all ingredients at room temperature. Preheat over to 350 degrees.

peach yogurt filling

2 pounds yogurt cheese, after draining from 3 32-ounce containers
8 ounces cream cheese, room temperature
½ cup sugar
½ cup brown sugar
1 tablespoon cornstarch
2 teaspoons vanilla extract
1 teaspoon lemon extract
1 tablespoon peach flavoring
1 teaspoon butter flavoring
¾ cup peaches (fresh or canned), mashed (2 medium)
2 envelopes unflavored gelatin, dissolved in ⅓ cup boiling water
4 egg whites, from large eggs
2 eggs
1 envelope whipped topping mix
⅓ cup sugar

In a large bowl, combine yogurt cheese and cream cheese, add ½ cup sugar, brown sugar, and cornstarch using an electric mixer. Beat until smooth and creamy. Stir in vanilla and lemon extracts and peach and butter flavorings. Stir in mashed peaches. Continue stirring until mixture is well blended. Stir completely dissolved gelatin into mixture. Set aside. In a large bowl, beat egg whites, whole eggs, and whipped topping mix with an electric mixer until mixture starts to thicken. Slowly add ⅓ cup sugar while beating. Beat until mixture thickens; this should take about 4–5 minutes. Do not double the volume. Stir egg mixture into batter until well blended. Pour batter onto crust. Bake at 350 degrees for 15 minutes.

REDUCE HEAT TO 200 DEGREES and bake for 2 hours, or until center is firm and no longer looks wet or shiny. Remove cake from oven and carefully run a knife around inside edge of pan. Turn oven off and return cake to it for an additional 2 hours. Chill overnight.

easy peach topping
¼ cup cold milk
1 teaspoon peach flavoring
1 envelope whipped topping mix
¼ cup peaches, mashed
¼ cup pecans, chopped

In a small bowl, beat milk, peach flavoring, and whipped topping mix with an electric mixer until thickened. Fold in mashed peaches. Spread topping over cake. Garnish with pecans. Keep chilled.

Per 1½-inch slice—Calories: 309 ♥ Fat: 15g ♥ Cholesterol: 64mg ♥ Protein: 8g ♥ Carbohydrates: 30g

PINEAPPLE YOGURT CREME CHEESECAKE

Make yogurt cheese (p. 235).

lemon cookie crust

18 lemon sandwich creme filled cookies, with fillings intact
5 tablespoons butter or margarine, softened

Crush cookies to make crumbs. Place crumbs in a mixing bowl and add butter, mix well. Press crumb mixture evenly onto bottom of greased 9-inch cheesecake pan. Set aside.

Have all ingredients at room temperature. Preheat over to 350 degrees.

pineapple yogurt filling

2 pounds yogurt cheese, after draining from 3 32-ounce containers
8 ounces cream cheese, room temperature
1 cup sugar
1 tablespoon cornstarch
2 teaspoons vanilla extract
2 teaspoons pineapple flavoring
2 teaspoons butter flavoring
20-ounce can crushed pineapple, well drained (reserve ¼ cup for topping)
2 envelopes unflavored gelatin, dissolved in ⅓ cup boiling water
4 egg whites, from large eggs
2 eggs
1 envelope whipped topping mix
⅓ cup sugar

In a large bowl, combine yogurt cheese and cream cheese, add 1 cup sugar and cornstarch using an electric mixer. Beat until smooth and creamy. Stir in vanilla extract and pineapple and butter flavorings.

274

Stir in drained pineapple and continue stirring until mixture is well blended. Stir completely dissolved gelatin into mixture. Set aside. In a large bowl, beat egg whites, whole eggs, and whipped topping mix with an electric mixer until mixture starts to thicken. Slowly add ⅓ cup sugar while beating. Beat until mixture thickens; this should take about 4–5 minutes. Do not double the volume. Stir egg mixture into batter until well blended. Pour batter onto crust. Bake at 350 degrees for 15 minutes.

REDUCE HEAT TO 200 DEGREES and bake for 2 hours, or until center is firm and no longer looks wet or shiny. Remove cake from oven and carefully run a knife around inside edge of pan. Turn oven off and return cake to it for an additional 2 hours. Chill overnight.

easy pineapple topping

¼ cup cold milk
1 teaspoon pineapple flavoring
1 envelope whipped topping mix
¼ cup crushed pineapple, well drained (from ingredients above)

In a small bowl, beat milk, pineapple flavoring, and whipped topping mix with an electric mixer until thickened. Fold in pineapple. Spread topping over cake. Keep chilled.

Per 1½-inch slice—Calories: 307 ♥ Fat: 15g ♥ Cholesterol: 64mg ♥ Protein: 8g ♥ Carbohydrates: 31g

STRAWBERRY YOGURT WITH CREME CHEESECAKE

Make yogurt cheese (p. 235).

vanilla cookie crust

18 vanilla sandwich creme filled cookies, with fillings intact
5 tablespoons butter or margarine, softened

Crush cookies to make fine crumbs. Place crumbs in a mixing bowl and add butter, mix well. Press crumb mixture evenly onto bottom of greased 9-inch cheesecake pan. Set aside.

Have all ingredients at room temperature. Preheat over to 350 degrees.

strawberry yogurt filling

2 pounds yogurt cheese, after draining from 3 32-ounce containers
8 ounces cream cheese, room temperature
1¼ cups sugar
1 tablespoon cornstarch
2 teaspoons vanilla extract
1 teaspoon lemon extract
1 tablespoon strawberry flavoring
1 cup strawberries (fresh or frozen), mashed
2 envelopes unflavored gelatin, dissolved in ⅓ cup boiling water
2 drops red food coloring
4 egg whites, from large eggs
2 eggs
1 envelope whipped topping mix
⅓ cup sugar

i ♥ cheesecake

In a large bowl, combine yogurt cheese and cream cheese, add 1¼ cups sugar and cornstarch using an electric mixer. Beat until smooth and creamy. Stir in vanilla and lemon extracts and strawberry flavoring. Stir in mashed strawberries. Continue stirring until mixture is well blended. Stir completely dissolved gelatin into mixture. Stir in red food coloring. Set aside. In a large bowl, beat egg whites, whole eggs, and whipped topping mix with an electric mixer until mixture starts to thicken. Slowly add ⅓ cup sugar while beating. Beat until mixture thickens; this should take about 4–5 minutes. Do not double the volume. Stir egg mixture into batter until well blended. Pour batter onto crust. Bake at 350 degrees for 15 minutes.

REDUCE HEAT TO 200 DEGREES and bake for 2 hours, or until center is firm and no longer looks wet or shiny. Remove cake from oven and carefully run a knife around inside edge of pan. Turn oven off and return cake to it for an additional 2 hours. Chill overnight.

easy strawberry topping

¼ cup cold milk
1 teaspoon strawberry flavoring
1 envelope whipped topping mix
strawberries, sliced
¼ cup pecans or walnuts, chopped
chocolate ice cream topping (the type that forms a hardened shell)

In a small bowl, beat milk, strawberry flavoring, and whipped topping mix with an electric mixer until thickened. Spread topping over cake. Garnish with strawberries, pecans or walnuts, and ice cream topping. Keep chilled.

Per 1½-inch slice—Calories: 285 ♥ Fat: 14g ♥ Cholesterol: 67mg ♥ Protein: 8g ♥ Carbohydrates: 32g

TURTLE YOGURT PECAN CHEESECAKE

Make yogurt cheese (p. 235).

chocolate wafer crust

8 ounces chocolate wafers

5 tablespoons butter or margarine, softened

Crush cookies to make crumbs. Place crumbs in a mixing bowl and add butter, mix well. Press crumb mixture evenly onto bottom of greased 9-inch cheesecake pan. Set aside.

Have all ingredients at room temperature. Preheat over to 350 degrees.

chocolate caramel yogurt filling

2 pounds yogurt cheese, after draining from 3 32-ounce containers

8 ounces cream cheese, room temperature

1¼ cups dark brown sugar

1 tablespoon cornstarch

⅓ cup dark corn syrup

2 teaspoons vanilla extract

2 teaspoons butter flavoring

8 ounces milk chocolate chips, melted

2 envelopes unflavored gelatin, dissolved in ⅓ cup boiling water

4 egg whites, from large eggs

2 eggs

1 envelope whipped topping mix

⅓ cup sugar

In a large bowl, combine yogurt cheese and cream cheese, add brown sugar and cornstarch using an electric mixer. Beat until smooth and creamy. Stir in corn syrup, vanilla extract, and butter flavoring. Stir in melted chocolate and continue stirring until mixture is well blended. Stir completely dissolved gelatin into mixture. Set aside. In a large bowl, beat egg whites, whole eggs, and whipped topping mix with an electric mixer until mixture starts to thicken. Slowly add ⅓ cup sugar while beating. Beat until mixture thickens; this should take about 4–5 minutes. Do not double the volume. Stir the egg mixture into the chocolate batter until well blended. Pour batter onto crust. Bake at 350 degrees for 15 minutes.

REDUCE HEAT TO 200 DEGREES and bake for 2 hours, or until center is firm and no longer looks wet or shiny. Remove cake from oven and carefully run a knife around inside edge of pan. Turn oven off and return cake to it for an additional 2 hours. Chill overnight.

chocolate caramel topping

4 ounces milk chocolate chips
¼ cup sour cream
caramel ice cream topping (the type that forms a hardened shell)
pecan halves

In a small heavy saucepan, melt chocolate chips and sour cream over low heat, stirring constantly until melted and smooth. Spread topping over cake. Drizzle caramel ice cream topping over cake, creating a design. Garnish with pecan halves. Keep chilled.

Per 1½-inch slice—Calories: 407 ♥ Fat: 15g ♥ Cholesterol: 68mg ♥ Protein: 9g ♥ Carbohydrates: 45g

VANILLA MARBLED YOGURT CHEESECAKE

Make yogurt cheese (p. 235).

chocolate cookie crust

18 chocolate sandwich creme filled cookies, with fillings intact
5 tablespoons butter or margarine, softened

Crush cookies to make fine crumbs. Place crumbs in a mixing bowl and add butter, mix well. Press crumb mixture evenly onto bottom of greased 9-inch cheesecake pan. Set aside.

Have all ingredients at room temperature. Preheat over to 350 degrees.

vanilla chocolate yogurt filling

2 pounds yogurt cheese, after draining from 3 32-ounce containers
8 ounces cream cheese, room temperature
1½ cups sugar
1 tablespoon cornstarch
¼ cup vanilla extract, or vanilla flavored liqueur
2 envelopes unflavored gelatin, dissolved in ⅓ cup boiling water
4 egg whites, from large eggs
2 eggs
1 envelope whipped topping mix
⅓ cup sugar
6 ounces milk chocolate chips, melted

In a large bowl, combine yogurt cheese and cream cheese, add 1½ cups sugar and cornstarch using an electric mixer. Beat until smooth and creamy. Stir in vanilla extract. Stir completely dissolved gelatin into mixture. Set aside. In a large bowl, beat egg whites, whole eggs, and whipped topping mix

i ♥ cheesecake

with an electric mixer until mixture starts to thicken. Slowly add ⅓ cup sugar while beating. Beat until mixture thickens; this should take about 4–5 minutes. Do not double the volume. Stir egg mixture into batter until well blended. Remove 1 cup batter and, in a small bowl, combine it with the melted chocolate. Set this aside. Pour half of batter onto crust. Spread half of chocolate batter over plain batter. Pour remaining plain batter over chocolate covered batter. Spread remaining chocolate batter over plain batter. Swirl the handle of a knife through the batter in a circular motion to create a marbling effect. Bake at 350 degrees for 15 minutes.

REDUCE HEAT TO 200 DEGREES and bake for 2 hours, or until center is firm and no longer looks wet or shiny. Remove cake from oven and carefully run a knife around inside edge of pan. Turn oven off and return cake to it for an additional 2 hours. Chill overnight.

chocolate whipped topping

¼ cup milk, very cold
1 envelope whipped topping mix
1 tablespoon cocoa
1 tablespoon powdered sugar
1 teaspoon vanilla extract
chocolate ice cream topping (the type that forms a hardened shell) (optional)

In a medium bowl, beat milk, whipped topping mix, cocoa, powdered sugar, and vanilla extract with an electric mixer until thickened and fluffy. Spread topping over cake. After chilling, drizzle chocolate ice cream topping over cake, creating a design. Keep chilled.

Per 1½-inch slice—Calories: 354 ♥ Fat: 15g ♥ Cholesterol: 64mg ♥ Protein: 8g ♥ Carbohydrates: 40g

VANILLA YOGURT CHEESECAKE

Make yogurt cheese (p. 235).

vanilla wafer crust

8 ounces vanilla wafers
5 tablespoons butter or margarine, softened

Crush cookies to make fine crumbs. Place crumbs in a mixing bowl and add butter, mix well. Press crumb mixture evenly onto bottom of greased 9-inch cheesecake pan. Set aside.

Have all ingredients at room temperature. Preheat over to 350 degrees.

vanilla yogurt filling

2 pounds yogurt cheese, after draining from 3 32-ounce containers
8 ounces cream cheese, room temperature
½ cup sour cream
1½ cups sugar
1 tablespoon cornstarch
¼ cup vanilla extract, or vanilla flavored liqueur
2 envelopes unflavored gelatin, dissolved in ⅓ cup boiling water
4 egg whites, from large eggs
2 eggs
1 envelope whipped topping mix
⅓ cup sugar

In a large bowl, combine yogurt cheese and cream cheese, add sour cream, 1½ cups sugar, and corn-starch using an electric mixer. Beat until smooth and creamy. Stir in vanilla extract. Stir completely dissolved gelatin into mixture. Set aside. In a large bowl, beat egg whites, whole eggs, and whipped

i ♥ cheesecake

topping mix with an electric mixer until mixture starts to thicken. Slowly add ⅓ cup sugar while beating. Beat until mixture thickens; this should take about 4–5 minutes. Do not double the volume. Stir egg mixture into batter until well blended. Pour batter onto crust. Bake at 350 degrees for 15 minutes.

REDUCE HEAT TO 200 DEGREES and bake for 2 hours, or until center is firm and no longer looks wet or shiny. Remove cake from oven and carefully run a knife around inside edge of pan. Turn oven off and return cake to it for an additional 2 hours. Chill overnight.

white chocolate topping

4 ounces white chocolate, melted
¼ cup sour cream
1 teaspoon vanilla extract
chocolate ice cream topping (the type that forms a hardened shell) (optional)

In a small heavy saucepan, melt chocolate and sour cream over low heat, stirring constantly until melted and smooth. Stir in vanilla extract. Spread topping over cake. After chilling, drizzle chocolate ice cream topping over cake, creating a design. Keep chilled.

Per 1½-inch slice — Calories: 337 ♥ Fat: 17g ♥ Cholesterol: 65mg ♥ Protein: 8g ♥ Carbohydrates: 37g

WHITE CHOCOLATE YOGURT CHEESECAKE

Make yogurt cheese (p. 235).

vanilla wafer crust

8 ounces vanilla wafers
5 tablespoons butter or margarine, softened

Crush cookies to make fine crumbs. Place crumbs in a mixing bowl and add butter, mix well. Press crumb mixture evenly onto bottom of greased 9-inch cheesecake pan. Set aside.

Have all ingredients at room temperature. Preheat over to 350 degrees.

white chocolate vanilla yogurt filling

2 pounds yogurt cheese, after draining from 3 32-ounce containers
8 ounces cream cheese, room temperature
1 cup sugar
1 tablespoon cornstarch
¼ cup vanilla extract, or vanilla flavored liqueur
12 ounces white chocolate, melted
2 envelopes unflavored gelatin, dissolved in ⅓ cup boiling water
4 egg whites, from large eggs
2 eggs
1 envelope whipped topping mix
¼ cup sugar

In a large bowl, combine yogurt cheese and cream cheese, add 1 cup sugar and cornstarch using an electric mixer. Beat until smooth and creamy. Stir in vanilla extract. Stir white chocolate into mixture. Stir completely dissolved gelatin into mixture. Set aside. In a large bowl, beat egg whites, whole eggs, and whipped topping mix with an electric mixer until mixture starts to thicken. Slowly add ¼ cup sugar while beating. Beat until mixture thickens; this should take about 4–5 minutes. Do not double the volume. Stir egg mixture into batter until well blended. Pour batter onto crust. Bake at 350 degrees for 15 minutes.

REDUCE HEAT TO 200 DEGREES and bake for 2 hours, or until center is firm and no longer looks wet or shiny. Remove cake from oven and carefully run a knife around inside edge of pan. Turn oven off and return cake to it for an additional 2 hours. Chill overnight.

white chocolate topping

4 ounces white chocolate
¼ cup sour cream
1 teaspoon vanilla extract
chocolate ice cream topping (the type that forms a hardened shell) (optional)
¼ cup pecans (optional)

In a small heavy saucepan, melt chocolate and sour cream over low heat, stirring constantly until melted and smooth. Stir in vanilla extract. Spread topping over cake. Drizzle chocolate ice cream topping over cake, creating a design, if desired. Sprinkle with pecans, if desired. Keep chilled.

Per 1½-inch slice—Calories: 408 ♥ Fat: 22g ♥ Cholesterol: 65mg ♥ Protein: 8g ♥ Carbohydrates: 43g

notes

index

Crust, filling, and topping indexes appear after the main index.

MAIN INDEX

i ♥ cheesecake

CRUSTS

FILLINGS

TOPPINGS